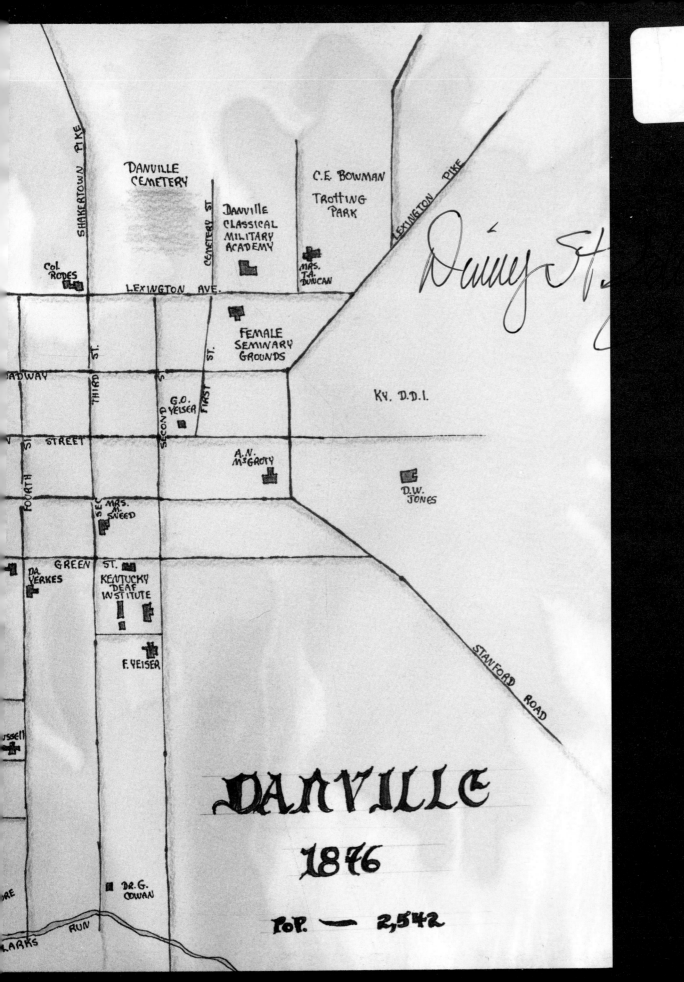

SHAKERTOWN PIKE

DANVILLE
CEMETERY

C.E. BOWMAN

TROTTING
PARK

LEXINGTON PIKE

DANVILLE
CLASSICAL
MILITARY
ACADEMY

MRS.
T.A.
DUNCAN

Col.
RODES

LEXINGTON AVE.

CEMETERY ST.

FEMALE
SEMINARY
GROUNDS

THIRD ST.

FIRST ST.

JADWAY

KY. D.D.I.

G.O.
YEISER

SECOND

V ST.

STREET

A.N.
McGROTY

D.W.
JONES

FOURTH

SE

MRS.
M.
SNEED

GREEN ST.

DA.
YERKES

KENTUCKY
DEAF
INSTITUTE

F. YEISER

STANFORD ROAD

SSELL

DANVILLE

1876

DR. G.
COWAN

RUN

LARKS

POP. — 2,542

Danville

AND BOYLE COUNTY

IN THE BLUEGRASS REGION IN KENTUCKY

An Architectural History

HEART OF DANVILLE BOOK COMMITTEE

TURNER PUBLISHING COMPANY
412 Broadway • P.O. Box 3101
Paducah, Kentucky 42002-3101
(270) 443-0121

Copyright © 1999 Heart of Danville Main Street
Program Book Committee
Publishing Rights: Turner Publishing Company
This book or any part thereof may not be
reproduced without the written consent of the
Heart of Danville Main Street Program
and Turner Publishing.

Turner Publishing Company Staff:
Keith R. Steele, Publishing Consultant
Pamela Wood, Project Coordinator
Shelley R. Davidson, Designer

Library of Congress Catalog Card No. 99-67626
ISBN: 1-56311-534-4

Printed on acid free paper in the
United States of America.
Additional copies may be purchased
from Heart of Danville.
Limited Edition.

The information used in this publication was
funded in part by grants from the National Park
Service, U.S. Department of the Interior,
administered by the Kentucky Heritage Council.
The use of federal funds does not imply
endorsement of the content by the
National Park Service or the
Kentucky Heritage Council.

Cover: *Forest Hill. c. 1814. KY 34 E. A late Georgian/early Federal house, originally a square one-story dwelling constructed by Rev. Samuel K. Nelson, a leading clergyman. Ordained in 1810, he became the pastor of the First Presbyterian Church in Danville and was active in the founding of the Kentucky School for the Deaf. NRL*

Back cover: *McClure-Barbee House. 304 South Fourth St., Danville. Built before 1850 by Robert Russel, Jr., for Samuel P. Barbee. Now serves as the home of the Heart of Danville, the Danville-Boyle County Chamber of Commerce, Boyle County Convention and Visitors Bureau, Boyle County Industrial Foundation, and the Boyle County Community Development Council. NRL*

Page 1: *William Thompson House. c.1800. Located off US 68 near the Mercer County line. This two-story, three room, stone structure has a central entry sheltered by a wide porch. It is an unusual bank-sited house, three-room plan with corner fireplaces. Includes an early basement level stone kitchen wing. Constructed on the 2000-acre land grant of William Thompson. During the Battle of Perryville, the house was used as a hospital. NRL*

Page 3: *H.P.Bottom House. Old Mackville Road, Perryville. A modest one and a half story weatherboard over log dog-trot farmhouse. Built in the early 1800's. Situated at the crossing of a main north-south road and strategic stream, the Bottom House marked the center of some of the heaviest fighting at the Battle of Perryville, on October 8, 1862. NRL*

Credits

Forest Hill with sheep.

Authors:	Mary Jo Joseph Janet Hamner
Cover Design:	Janet Hamner
Photo Editing:	Mary Jo Joseph Janet Hamner
Consultant:	Donna Logsdon
Photography:	Brad Simmons Photography Wilma Brown Janet Hamner John Gentry
Illustration:	A. Jack May
Maps:	Mack Jackson

Russel-Thomas House. *c.1850. 101 Maple Avenue, Danville.   A Greek Revival, seven bay brick with low-pitched roof and large pedimented portico with Doric columns. The home was built and occupied by Robert Russel, Jr.   NRL*

Contents

The Clock Barn was an extraordinary partially log structure with hay hoods projecting from each end and a central tower with a clock in each of four sides. It served as a landmark on the Lebanon Road on the southwest side of Danville for almost 100 years, and was razed when the Minor farm became part of the industrial area in late 1996.

Acknowledgements

For support, encouragement and advocacy, for loan of precious materials, and for cooperation and patience, the Book Committee thanks the following:

- Heart of Danville Boards and Staffs, past and present.

- Property owners and all others who shared their photos and histories.

- David Morgan and the Kentucky Heritage Council for funding and guidance.

- Old House Club, for making possible the surveying and establishment of the historic districts in Danville.

- Cecil Dulin Wallace for her vision of what Perryville might one day be and for her dedication to preservation throughout the county as administered through the Boyle Landmark Trust.

- George and Nell Grider for contributions made to the early restoration of the McDowell House and Apothecary Shop.

- Chris Amos, Gibson Worsham, Helen Powell, and Mary Breeding for research and survey.

Thanks also for the enthusiasm and confidence of all who bought this book prior to publication.

Cambus Kenneth Farm. *Antebellum brick icehouse with office above.*

Dedication

In memory of Cecil Dulin Wallace, who taught us the love and lore of our communities and instilled in us the importance of preserving our rich architectural heritage.

Robert Walker House *This house was built about 1832 and was used as a hospital during and after the Battle of Perryville. It sits on a farm located between Battlefield Road and US 68.*

Introduction

Boyle County and its principal city and seat of government, Danville, lie in the most beautiful rolling countryside of all of central Kentucky. Before the area was settled, however, it was described as "a howling wilderness," covered with forests and great canebrakes. But early settlers, many of whom were displaced from their homelands by laws of primogeniture, could readily see how vast and rich was the land.

Present-day Danville and Boyle County probably saw its first settlers in 1774. In that year Pennsylvanian James Harrod and a party of settlers journeyed down the Monongahela and Ohio Rivers and up the Kentucky River to "Oregon Landing," establishing Harrodsburg near the Salt River, the first permanent white settlement west of the Allegheny Mountains. Harrod's men "scattered in small companies to select locations" to improve lands and build cabins. Among them were Harrod's brother, Thomas Harrod, along with John Crow, James Brown, Jared Cowan, Isaac Hite and brothers James and Silas Harlan, all whom claimed lands in present-day Boyle County. Thomas Harrod improved the lands surrounding the great sinking spring on what is now the Centre College campus in 1774. John Crow may have erected on the land he claimed the first log cabin in what became the City of Danville that same year. The Harlans improved lands along the Salt River.

In the early years of Kentucky's settlement, sturdy Scottish-Irish settlers from present-day Augusta, Rockbridge and Botetourt Counties in the Upper Shenandoah Valley of Virginia were lured to this region by the rich lands and abundant sources of water found here. What enabled those settlers to actually reach what is now Boyle County and Danville, as well as Perryville, was the great Wilderness Road. The Wilderness Road was opened up in the late Spring of 1775, several months after the North Carolina-based Transylvania Company, with the assistance of a woodsman named Daniel Boone, "purchased" all of the lands south of the Kentucky River from the Cherokee Indians during a questionable private treaty-signing at a gathering place along the Watauga River, known as Sycamore Shoals.

Following an ancient buffalo trace which led through the Cumberland Gap, Daniel Boone and a party of Transylvania Company axmen blazed a trail northwestward from the southeastern Kentucky highlands and along the north-south "Warrior's Trace" to the south bank of the Kentucky River near Otter Creek at a place which they named Boonesboro. At a site called the Hazel Patch, just north of present-day London, Kentucky, the first branch of the Wilderness Road was begun. There, in April, 1775, Colonel Benjamin Logan and a party of hunters and axmen from Virginia left Boone's trace and improved a series of obscure trails running westward in order to explore the region of and beyond the Dick's River. Logan established a fort and settlement in present-day Lincoln County, known as St.

Asaph's or Logan's Station, and he and his settlers then helped extend the westward trail to Harrodsburg, and ultimately to the Falls of the Ohio at present-day Louisville. That extension of the Wilderness Road (which generally follows present-day U.S. Route 150 and includes Danville's Main Street) ultimately bore the family name of three Irish-born "Long Hunters," Henry, Charles and Richard Skaggs, who, it was said, first roughly marked out the paths Logan followed.

It was "Skaggs's Trace" that enabled those Shenandoah Valley settlers to reach present-day Boyle County in great numbers during and after the Revolutionary War. Illustrative of how desirable these lands were then, at least seven pioneer "stations," or stockaded blockhouses, were erected within or near present-day Danville by 1780: John Crow's, William Fields's, James Lawrence's, John Reed's, George Clark's, John Dougherty's, and Stephen Fisher's. Despite frequent Indian raids and attacks during and after the Revolution, stockaded blockhouses were erected in the area by Virginia families bearing the names Irvin, Harlan, Caldwell and Cowan.

All of Kentucky then was part of Virginia. What became Boyle County was then within Lincoln County, Virginia, one of three counties of the Old Dominion comprising Kentucky. That was soon to change. Shortly after the District of Kentucky was created by the Virginia legislature in 1783, the site of the "Supreme Court" for the district was established here at Crow's Station. One of those settlers who had arrived at Crow's Station was Walker Daniel. A lawyer of significant accomplishment, Daniel became the first Attorney General for the District of Kentucky, and it was he who was instrumental in moving the Supreme Court from Harrodsburg to what is now Danville. John Crow then conveyed to Daniel a parcel of land within a "rich, undulating plain" between Clark's Run and Wilson's Run in 1784. Tragically, Daniel was killed by the Indians near Bullitt's Lick on August 12 of that same year. Upon Daniel's land, though, was laid out the City of Danville. It is likely the city was named for Walker Daniel.

Because it became the seat of justice for the District of Kentucky and was situated along Skaggs's Trace, Danville grew rapidly. More western Virginians, traveling Skaggs's Trace, poured into the area in the years following the Revolution. Scottish-Irish settlers from the Upper Shenandoah Valley, bearing names like McDowell, Barbee, McClure, McClung, McGrorty, McIlvoy and McKee, claimed and improved lands in and near Danville.

With the completion of a log court house and jail in 1785 came taverns for the travelers attending court sessions. Most of the early taverns were located near the court house square or along Skaggs's Trace. Benjamin Grayson's Tavern was the first in 1785. The tavern Grayson built in 1800 still stands. Gill's Tavern followed. Jeremiah Clemens built a tavern nearby in 1793. Then, in 1799, Richard Davenport built a tavern and inn. The Virginia legislature, recognizing the growth and importance of the town, finally incorporated the City of Danville in 1787. It was to prove to be a parting gesture by the Old Dominion, though.

In Danville, the Commonwealth of Kentucky was actually given birth. Because of its location and early importance as the seat of justice, Danville became the site of a series of conventions of the settlers of the District of Kentucky, called for the purpose of separating the three counties which comprised what was then Kentucky — Lincoln, Fayette and Jefferson — from Virginia. The first convention was called by none other than Colonel Benjamin Logan in an effort to simply organize all of the settlements for defense against Indian raids; the convention ended calling for separation from Virginia. In the end, ten successive conventions met at the log court house in Danville between 1784 and 1792. The first eight conventions sought separation. The Ninth Convention was called to accept Virginia's final terms of separation, and the Tenth Convention, which met in early April, 1792, "framed and adopted" Kentucky's first constitution. Presiding at those conventions was Samuel McDowell of Danville, one of the first judges of the Supreme Court of the District of Kentucky. McDowell's judicial career continued with Kentucky's statehood. His "neighbor," Revolutionary War hero Isaac Shelby, became Kentucky's first governor. Here in Danville was Kentucky's political beginning.

With statehood, Kentucky's capital was moved to Lexington, but Danville prospered nonetheless. It became the site of Kentucky's first post office in 1792 (which still stands), numerous dry goods stores, a bank and even a cotton factory, known as the "Kentucky Manufacturing Company," and an apothecary shop. One dry goods store was owned by James Birney, who each year traveled all the way to Philadelphia to buy merchandise, hauling it back to Danville by wagons, pulled by ox teams. Noted silversmiths like Samuel Ayres and, much later, J.B. Akin, practiced their craft here. Ayres's frame shop still occupies its space on Main Street. Churches, of course, came with the early settlers. The Scottish-Irish settlers were largely Presbyterian. Not surprisingly, they, led by "Father" David Rice, built the first meeting house in Danville in 1784. Episcopalians, Methodists, Baptists and others followed. One of Kentucky's first public libraries was organized in Danville as early as 1800, evidence of the refinement of, and the importance of education to, the town's early settlers. And, in Danville, Judge Samuel McDowell's Scottish-educated son, Dr. Ephraim McDowell, performed the world's first ovariotomy on young Jane Todd Crawford on Christmas Day, 1809. Interestingly, both Dr. McDowell and Jane Todd Crawford were born in present-day Rockbridge County, Virginia, not more than fifteen miles apart.

In 1819, a committee of distinguished Danville citizens, led by none other than Kentucky's first governor, Isaac Shelby, whose lovely home, "Traveler's Rest," stood nearby, incorporated Centre College in Danville, a school which would always be strongly identified with the Presbyterian roots of the town. Shelby was named the first Chairman of Centre's Board of Trustees. Centre College quickly grew to become one of the very fine colleges in the nation. It would produce two Vice Presidents of the United States, John C. Breckinridge and Adlai Stevenson; Chief Justice of the United States Fred Moore Vinson; Associate Justice of the Supreme Court of the United States John Marshall Harlan; fourteen United States Senators; nearly forty-five Congressmen; a dozen State Governors; thirty-one college presidents; and nearly one hundred state and federal judges. In 1822, Danville became the site of the first state-established school for the deaf in the nation. Like Centre College, the Kentucky School for the Deaf is a centerpiece of present-day Danville and Boyle County.

Boyle County was created in 1842 when the state legislature carved it out from parts of Lincoln and Mercer Counties. It was named for John Boyle, a Botetourt County, Virginia native, Jeffersonian congressman from Kentucky, and the Chief Justice of Kentucky from 1810 to 1827. The county name was apt, for Justice Boyle and his family would play vital roles in the growth of Danville and Boyle County throughout the nineteenth century.

From an eighteenth century village of mostly rough, log houses and public buildings (some of which still remain), Danville grew to reflect the prosperity and refinement of the first half of the nineteenth century, as many of its houses and buildings built in those years were constructed of brick or clapboard and imitated the Federal-style architecture then popular in Virginia. Many Federal-style private homes of substantial citizens here sported ornamental fan doorways and gracious porticos. Some of those houses proudly stand today. In the years before the Civil War, Greek Revival houses, with giant Doric or Ionic columns, supporting graceful porticos or long porches, and even a number of Gothic-Revival homes similar to those popular in the Hudson River Valley of New York, dotted the towns of Danville and Perryville and the countryside of Boyle County. Many of the houses built in the years just before the Civil War, still grace the area. In 1831 the Episcopalians, led by none other than Dr. Ephraim McDowell, built the lovely brick Trinity Church on Main Street; the Presbyterians completed the beautiful, brick, Gothic-style First Presbyterian Church near Centre College that same year. Both churches ornament Main Street today. By the outbreak of the war, Boyle County completed a handsome brick, Greek Revival court house; it stands now as the local center of justice on Main Street.

In the years before the Civil War, the agitation over slavery was deeply felt in Danville and Boyle County. The area was dominated by slaveholders whose ancestors had brought the slave institution with them over Skaggs's Trace. Yet, here, the debate took what we might think today to be odd forms. Some slaveowners favored protecting slavery from federal interference, but opposed secession. Others opposed slavery, but also opposed federal interference and immediate abolition. There were few radical abolitionists. One prominent abolitionist, James Gillespie Birney, son of James Birney of Danville, and a founder of Centre College, sought redress without the radicalism of the New England abolitionists. The Birney homestead, "Woodlawn," still remains at the end of its long tree-lined lane just west of Danville. Centre College, like the Presbyterian Church, faced contentious debates over slavery. Noted Centre President John C. Young sided with the antislavery faculty and administration of the college, but steered the institution along a moderate and amiable path. After his death and, as a result of the Civil War, Centre College, like its mother church, actually suffered bitter division.

Although dominated by slaveowners, some of whose hearts may well have favored the cause of secession, Boyle County and Danville, like Kentucky in general, never had the opportunity to fully advance that sentiment. After a tumultuous legislative session and only five weeks after the firing on Fort Sumter, Kentucky's Governor Beriah Magoffin declared the State "neutral" in May, 1861. Following the August legislative elections that year, Gen. William "Bull" Nelson, with the blessing of President Abraham Lincoln, set up a Union recruiting and training base between the Kentucky and Dick's Rivers, at a site in Garrard County called Hoskins's Cross Roads and known as Camp Dick Robinson. Established to raise and train Union troops to seize pro-Union East Tennessee, its presence breached Kentucky's "neutrality" and quickly brought nearby Boyle County and Danville under Union control. With the Confederate withdrawal from Kentucky after the Battle of Mill Springs and the fall of Forts Henry and Donelson in the Winter of 1862, Union control of the State was complete. That domination was broken only once, and that was with the Confederate invasion of Kentucky in the Summer and Fall of 1862 which ended tragically just west of Perryville in Boyle County when Gen. Braxton Bragg's Confederate Army of the Mississippi, 25,000 strong, and Gen. Don Carlos Buell's Union Army of the Ohio, nearly 54,000 strong, fought across those rolling fields alongside the Chaplin River on October 8, 1862 for more than five hours, suffering combined casualties of nearly 8,000. It was the bloodiest day in Kentucky's history, and the signs of it in Union and Confederate gravesites in public and private cemeteries and on blood-stained floors of ante-bellum houses and public buildings used as hospitals may be found throughout Perryville, Danville, and Boyle County to this day.

Not surprisingly, in the end, Danville, Perryville, and Boyle County became largely pro-Union, although there were a surprising number of Confederates who hailed from the area. A number of Union regiments were partly mustered out of Boyle County. Unquestionably, Boyle County's most noted Civil War personalities were pre-war lawyers and Union officers: Colonel John Marshall Harlan, by then a lawyer in Louisville who became a brigade commander; General Speed Smith Fry, a local lawyer, who, it was said, fired the shot at the Battle of Mill Springs that killed General Felix K. Zollicoffer, and who became commander of Camp Nelson in Jessamine County in 1863; and General Jeremiah Tilford Boyle (Judge Boyle's son), another local lawyer, who commanded a brigade at the Battle of Shiloh and became Commander of the Union Military District of Kentucky. Interestingly, General Fry's adversary at the Battle of Mill Springs, Confederate General George Bibb Crittenden, moved to Danville after the war and died here in 1880. Both Fry and Boyle are buried in Danville's lovely Belleview Cemetery. Crittenden was buried in Frankfort, Kentucky.

With peace restored, Danville, Perryville, and Boyle County, like other areas of Kentucky, turned to industry as well as agriculture to regenerate the area's economy. Roads were improved over time, and the railroads came to the area. The first railroad to enter Boyle County was the Louisville & Nashville Railroad which extended its spur line from Lebanon, Kentucky to Stanford during the last months of the Civil War. The idea for the line was first advanced during the war by General Boyle as a necessity for his military department. The line that was actually built did not enter Danville, but, instead, cut across southern Boyle County. The Cincinnati, New Orleans & Texas Pacific Railroad (later the Southern Railroad) completed its main north-south line through Danville by 1877, crossing the Louisville & Nashville at Junction City. Where once there was a cotton factory, Danville saw the construction and operation of hemp manufacturing companies, feed and grain mills, cut stone companies, and even the Riems Electric Clock Company before the turn of the century. Fancy Victorian houses appeared, and many may still be seen.

With the Twentieth Century, Danville and Boyle County advanced with the times. Its sons fought in two world wars, Korea and Vietnam. The Goodall Company, manufacturer of "Palm Beach" suits, opened a plant in Danville in 1937. The General Shoe Company opened its plant here ten years later. By the century's end, Matsushita Appliance Corporation, Hobart Corporation, American Greetings Corporation, R.R. Donnelley & Sons, Phillips Lighting Company and many others had opened facilities in Danville and Boyle County. With a fine hospital, appropriately named the Ephraim McDowell Medical Center, and several shopping centers, Danville and Boyle County met the needs of modern times.

Danville no longer stands along a great western road. In fact, the city is situated a great distance from any modern Interstate highway. It is not the center of justice of the Commonwealth any longer, nor is it the center of politics. Nevertheless, Danville, and its neighbor, Perryville, and Boyle County in general, retain a delightful combination of the old and new. With a notable history, the citizens of Danville, Perryville, and Boyle County proudly point to the fact that they have more historic houses, public buildings and sites listed on the National Register of Historic Places in this area than any other of comparable size and population in America. Even in this modern age, Danville's, Perryville's, and Boyle County's present-day homes and business establishments serenely co-exist with the area's historic structures. Along tree-shaded streets and lanes, they blend. One can see in all those properties the history and development of Danville, Perryville and Boyle County, and this wonderful book captures that story in photography and text. It is a most valuable contribution to the study of this beautiful and historic region.

Kent Masterson Brown
Danville, Kentucky

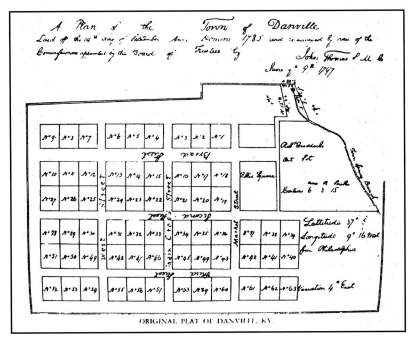

ORIGINAL PLAT OF DANVILLE, KY.

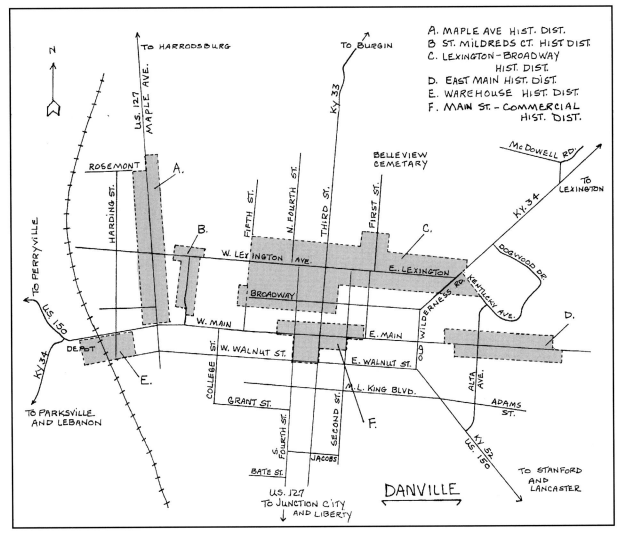

A. MAPLE AVE HIST. DIST.
B ST. MILDREDS CT. HIST. DIST.
C. LEXINGTON-BROADWAY HIST. DIST.
D. EAST MAIN HIST. DIST.
E. WAREHOUSE HIST. DIST.
F. MAIN ST.- COMMERCIAL HIST. DIST.

DANVILLE

Preface

In the Commonwealth, Boyle County has one of the largest concentrations of properties listed on the National Register of Historic Places. It is the intent of this publication to catalogue and give insight into our architectural wealth and to emphasize the importance of maintaining it.

We have been blessed, over time, with citizens who have worked tirelessly to remember and preserve our foundations for the benefit of future generations. We are privileged to follow them and hope that this book will inspire others to the same pride of place.

The Authors

Photos are captioned as follows:

NRL: Individually listed on the National Register of Historic Places.
NRHD: Included in a National Register Historic District.
NRS: Surveyed for possible nomination to the National Register of Historic Places.

National Register Identification numbers are included in the Index.

See maps pages 16 and 18.

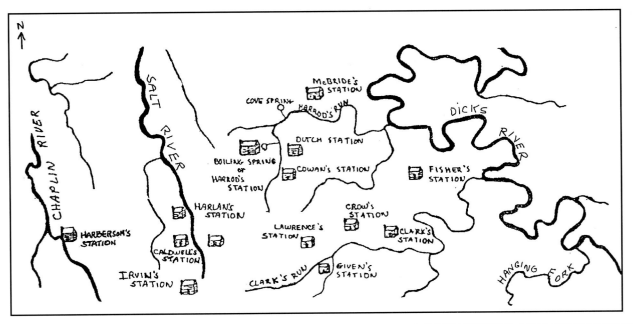

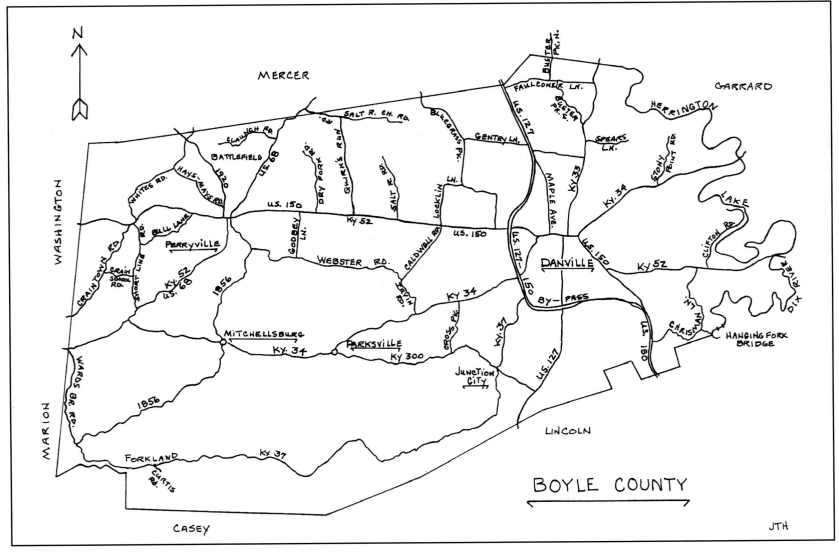

BOYLE COUNTY

JTH

CHAPTER I

Beginnings, 1774

When migration to Kentucky began in the 1770's, those hardy pioneers came primarily from Maryland, Pennsylvania, North Carolina and Virginia on land grants from the Revolutionary War or preemption claims. Following buffalo paths used by the Indians or floating down the Ohio River, men like James Harrod began a new chapter in the history of our young nation. They had been lured west by the irresistible stories of the abundance of wildlife, virgin forests and beautiful meadows.

Harrod and company came up the Kentucky River from the Ohio to the banks of a large spring on the Salt River near present day Harrodsburg in 1774. This democratic group of settlers drew lots for their parcels of land, and built shelters called "lottery cabins." James Crow happened to draw the area of present day downtown Danville and his basic fortification was near the Town Branch spring on today's East Broadway.

Rude cabins were built and the obligatory corn crop was planted to satisfy the requirements of their claims. Even though these were abandoned due to the call from Virginia to help in the Battle of Point Pleasant in late 1774, this was the beginning of the early "stations" fanning out from James Harrod's first fortification. After the battle and Indian attacks lessened, most of the company of men returned to start new life on the western frontier.

Danville and the smaller communities in present-day Boyle County trace their roots to these early stations established by Crow, Harlan, Caldwell, Harberson and others. From the late 18th century through the end of the 20th century, Danville and Boyle County have gained a reputation as a leader in the political, cultural, religious, educational and commercial arena of not only the Bluegrass region but the entire Commonwealth of Kentucky.

We have been fortunate that the pride of ownership and the historical events of this area have preserved the past for future generations. From the early log structures to the handsome residences and educational and religious institutions, our streetscapes and countryside tell the story of our community.

At left: *Reconstructed log structure. c.1780.* On the Clemens Caldwell Farm, Maple Avenue at Harrodsburg Road. Was moved from the Salt River Road, Harlan Station historic area.

Below: *First Post Office* west of the Alleghenies was this hand hewn log structure located on Walnut Street and moved in 1950 to Constitution Square State Park on Second Street. At other times, it was used as a residence and nurses' quarters for McDowell Hospital. NRL/NRHD

Post Office when located on Walnut Street, covered in weatherboarding.

CHAPTER II

Settlement, 1774-1820

The first permanent dwellings built at the stations and in Danville were made of log. These one and two room cabins were separated by a breezeway called a dog-trot. Later a gabled-end chimney and large fireplace would have been built to provide heat and cook the meals. To gain more room, the dog-trot would often be enclosed. Porches were added to catch summer breezes.

Two early log structures surviving from this period include the first post office west of the Allegheny Mountains and Grayson's Tavern, both in Constitution Square, and later covered in weatherboarding.

The largest collection of log and frame homes, many still occupied, is in the Perryville Historic District. Another one, painstakingly renovated, is the H.P. Bottom house near the Perryville Battlefield. Except for the post office, all the examples appear to be the dog-trot or hall-parlor plan.

Since there was an abundance of limestone in this area, the settlers often chose to build more secure and substantial dwellings of stone. The Crows, John and William, built two stone homes on a land grant south of their first station in present downtown Danville. Records indicate that John built his one room home about 1784 but it was purchased late that same year by General Thomas Barbee. Thomas and his son, Joshua, are credited with expanding this property into a massive two-story dry-laid stone house with Doric columns in the Greek Revival style. William Crow's two-story house begun about 1783, evolved into a stately Federal structure.

Another large area of settlement was that of the Harlan family on the Salt River north of US 150 West. Father and sons built several stone and, later, brick structures in the Federal style on both sides of the old road. Wilson's Station and the Marshall House, both on KY 34, and the William Thompson house off US 68 are the least changed and still occupied stone dwellings in the county.

The last phase of the settlement period changed dramatically with the introduction of brick as a building material for the predominantly Federal structures in the 1790's and early 1800's. With better economic stability, the pioneers began to fire brick from their own clay soil and sometimes import craftsmen from the East coast to build more elaborate dwellings with fine woodwork and detailing both on the interior and exterior. The Federal style architecture is rectangular and symmetrical in design with a central doorway surrounded by windows suggesting the central passage plan.

One of the most outstanding late Georgian and early Federal examples and rare in this region is "Forest Hill," a one story, three pavilion brick structure built in 1814 by Reverend Samuel Nelson.

Judge John Boyle, for whom the county is named, built his home about 1815. It is a one and one-half story Federal brick dwelling with projecting entry portico.

Naturally, most of the homes, churches and commercial buildings of this period exemplify characteristics of more than one style. As owners, finances and tastes changed, so did the structures.

Harlan Family Dwellings. *James, Silas, George, and Elijah Harlan came to Kentucky with James Harrod in 1774, and claimed land in the Salt River Road area. Between 1778 and 1781, there was intense development of stations in the Bluegrass region that were inhabited by settlers who worked clearing fields by day and retired to the safety of defensible forts by night. Stations were usually smaller than forts but were fortified and were landmarks where travelers could stop for shelter and food.*

Harlan's Station is a stone ruin on Salt River Road. The house was a two-story limestone residence with a corner fireplace, constructed in 1785 by James Harlan. One or two additions were constructed a short time later: a log ell and one-story shed porch. On or near the site of the house was a log station built in 1778 by James Harlan and his brother, Silas.

Located nearby and to the east, is an early brick 1 1/2 story house on 1000 acres of land, thought to have belonged to Elijah Harlan. It was purchased in 1822 from Silas Harlan by James Granville Cecil. It stayed in the Cecil family for over 100 years and was reportedly used as a headquarters for troops in the Battle of Perryville.

The Harlans and their descendants remained in this area for many years and several houses are attributed to them. Supreme Court Justice John Harlan was born here, served in the Union Army before serving on the Supreme Court from 1877 to 1911.

At right: *Abner Knox Farm.* c.1783 US 150 W. This house was one of the earliest stone houses in the area. It was built by David Knox, a stonemason from Philadelphia in 1783 in the Atoka area. A later occupant, Thomas Armstrong, fought for the Union in the Civil War and the house was used as a hospital during the Battle of Perryville. It was razed in the 1960's when the new Perryville Road was built. NRL

At left: *William Crow House.* c.1783. KY 52 E. A stone asymmetrical four bay, two-story home with a one-story stone wing. William was the brother of John and leader in the Presbyterian Church. NRL

Marshall House. c.1790. KY 34 W. One of only two known examples of Gothic Revival dry-laid stone houses in the state. NRL

At left: *John Barbee House.* c.1790. KY 34E. John Barbee and his six sons came to Kentucky from Culpepper County, Virginia prior to 1788 after they all served in the Revolutionary War. The stone house was built soon after their arrival in the Stoney Point area three miles north of Danville on the Lexington Road. Barbee, who died in 1805, and his sons played a prominent role in the early development of Danville. NRL

Above: *Crow-Barbee House.* Stanford Road, Danville. The main portion of this stone structure is considered to be the first stone house west of the Alleghenies. It was built about 1780 by John Crow. In 1784 another pioneer leader, General Thomas Barbee, purchased the property and between 1784-1792 added the wings and front porch. Thomas Barbee was the first postmaster. His sons, Joshua, helped found Centre College and, Elias, helped establish the Kentucky School for the Deaf. NRL

At left: Stone House on the old Lexington stagecoach road was built before 1800 by the Innis family and owned in the late 1800's by the Chinns. It is a three-bay, three-story home with exterior end chimneys. NRL.

At right and above: *"Dutch Barn"*. *c.1800. Spears Lane. This was probably built by Zachariah Smith. Smith was one of the German Lutherans who came to Kentucky with Stephen Fisher of "Fisher's Garrison". The house appears to be built in at least two periods with the first section to the south being stone. The north side, now the front, is log covered with weatherboarding. It is a five bay hall parlor plan with a semi-detached stone kitchen. NRL*

James Wilson House. c.1785. Wilson's Station "Cragfont", KY 34W. Located at the fork of Clark's Run. A large stone fortified structure. Garret vents flank the chimney in the attic and were probably used as gun ports during Indian attacks. NRL

Walker House. c.1810. 1 1/2 story, weatherboard over log with exterior stone chiminey. Located on Polk Street in the earliest section of Perryville. NRL

Rupley House. c.1820. N. Bragg Street, Perryville. A 1 1/2 story, three bay log house covered with weatherboarding, having brick chimneys at both ends. NRL

J.M.Gray House. c.1820. Fifth Street, Perryville. A one story, five bay frame on a stone foundation with two brick chimneys. NRL

Purdom – Lewis – Hutchinson House. *c.1790. Curtis Road. A log, dog-trot, with weatherboarding. One-story with semi-detached kitchen. NRL*

Early three-bay, one story frame dwelling with center chimney, US 150 W.

House on West Broadway, Danville. *One of two log homes on Broadway, built in the early 1800's and later covered by weatherboarding.*

Left and below: *Vermillion House and Farm.* c.1836. Salt River Church Road. Part of the Low Dutch settlement along the Salt River at the Mercer County line. Frame over log with stone end chimneys, one bearing the inscription "1836". The year "1839" is carved in the other. NRS

J.L. Walker House. c.1820. Fifth Street, Perryville. Front entry with transom and side lights. Located in section of town laid off in 1816. NRL

Cocanougher House. Bragg Street, Perryville. 1 1/2 story, five bay, with porch over the center three bays. This section of town was laid out in 1817. NRL

Dunlap House. c.1820. N. Third Street, Danville. Federal three bay log covered with weatherboarding. NRL/NRHD

Dr. William Harlan House, Chrisman Lane.. Early frame dwelling with many additions. NRS

At right: *John Braxdale House.* *c.1801.* *Bluegrass Pike.* *This two story Federal home was built by John B. Braxdale and his wife, the former Martha Ripperdan, on a 1000-acre estate inherited from his father. The elder Braxdale established a station known as Braxdale Spring in 1775. The house has been enlarged over the years and has been owned by the George Spears and Clyde Jackson families.*

Below: *Davenport House.* *c.1820.* *Smith Street, Perryville. Federal, 1 1/2 story, three bay brick on stone foundation with interior brick chimneys. The only one of its kind in Perryville. NRL*

Above and left: *Crawford – Finch – English – Sutcliff House.* *c.1790. US 150 W. This two story, three bay dwelling shows Greek Revival influences now but began its storied history as a log house in 1790. It has had several brick and frame additions and deletions. At one time, it had a wide porch covering the center bay with a balcony and second floor door above the entrance. It was the first house in the state to have tan-bark insulation and had one of the first copper bathtubs. A large spring on the 1800 acre farm attracted both Confederate and Union soldiers and the home sheltered the wounded after the battle. NRS*

Dr. Ephraim McDowell House and Apothecary Shoppe. c.1804. South Second Street, Danville. These pictures were taken before the property was purchased and restored by the Kentucky Medical Association in 1939. The Kentucky Pharmaceutical Association, led by George Grider, local pharmacist and historian, renovated the brick apothecary shop in 1955. It was also used as an early post office.

Dr. McDowell and Dr. Adam Rankin began their medical practice in the brick structure in 1795. McDowell purchased the frame dwelling in 1802 after his marriage to Sarah Shelby, daughter of Governor Isaac Shelby. In December 1809, Dr. McDowell performed the famous ovarian surgery on Jane Todd Crawford, establishing his title of "Father of Abdominal Surgery". NRL/NRHD

Caldwell House. *This 1 1/2 story Federal style house is located on the Parksville Crosspike and was in the Rodes family for many years.* NRS

Joseph McDowell House. *US 150 W. This early Federal style home with late nineteenth century additions of dormers and porch is attributed to Joseph McDowell, son of Samuel McDowell.* NRS

Harlan-Bruce House. *c.1815. This early photograph shows the house with its fine Federal portico long since removed. The land was purchased in 1794 by George Harlan from George Pope and the house constructed circa 1815. The Bruce family purchased it in 1844 and lived there until 1908. Len Bruce was co-owner of the "Kentucky Advocate".* NRL

Waveland – Willis Green House. c.1800. Erskine Drive, Danville. A four room, center hall plan which originally faced east. The present porch on the west side was added in 1914. Green represented Kentucky in the Virginia legislature and was an original trustee of Transylvania Academy and an influential member of the Danville Political Club. NRL

Samuel McDowell House. Pleasant Vale. c.1784. KY 34. A two story, five bay brick Federal house with a Greek Revival portico and pediment. Pleasant Vale was the home of the Samuel McDowell family from 1784 to 1845. Samuel, father of Dr. Ephraim McDowell, came from Virginia to be one of the first judges of the Kentucky District Court and president of the convention that framed the first constitution of Kentucky. Samuel also organized the Danville Political Club here in 1786 for the purpose of debating the controversial issues of the conventions leading to statehood in 1792. NRL

Hillcrest, on the Centre College Campus, was a Federal house with a Gothic Revival Porch. It was built as a dining hall after Old Centre was erected in 1820 and was used as the college president's home but was eventually razed.

At right: *Alban Goldsmith House.* c.1810. South Second Street, Danville. Dr. Goldsmith studied under Dr. McDowell and chartered the "Medical Institute" which became the University of Louisville School of Medicine. The house is much changed from its original appearance. NRL/NRHD

Below: *Daniel Yeiser House.* c.1823. KY 34. One and one half story dwelling with Palladin windows in a three bay facade. Dr. Yeiser gradually changed his vocation from physician to planter and was one of the founders of the Episcopal church in Danville. NRS

Webb House. c.1830. Buckner Street, Perryville. An early Federal style cottage. Three bay, 1 1/2 story frame on stone foundation. Chimneys have corbelled tops. NRL

Rice-Cowan House. c.1830. West Broadway, Danville. This frame and log Federal structure is one of few surviving log houses built prior to 1800 in the downtown area. It was probably built by Daniel McIlvoy in 1797 when he purchased one-quarter of the town. In 1832, John Jackson added two stories and four rooms to the dog-trot cabin that originally faced Fifth Street. A later owner, Dr. Fayette Montgomery, purchased the property in 1898 and in 1907 built a private hospital behind the house. NRL/NRHD

Above: *Fields House and Farm.* c.1820. Salt River Church Road. Two story, five bay frame with log portions. A Federal style home, in the Low Dutch settlement along the Salt River Church Road. NRS

At right: *Calvert Armstrong House.* c.1820. North Bragg Street in Perryville. A two story, asymmetrical three bay frame house built by Isaiah Calvert. One of the earliest structures in Perryville, used to house the injured after the Battle of Perryville. NRL

Bottom – McAfee - Guthrie House. *c.1820. West Fourth Street, Perryville. A two-story, three bay frame Federal style house with Greek Revival pediment and balcony supported by four large columns. And some handsome folks. NRL*

Frederick Ripperdan House, "Woodcock". *c.1791. Locklin Lane. The present Greek Revival style home was enlarged from the original 1791 log structure built by Frederick and Sarah Ripperdan. Ripperdan, a Revolutionary War soldier came to Fort Boonesborough from Virginia in 1780 and purchased this land from John Cowan in 1781. Their daughter, Martha, married John B. Braxdale. NRS*

Lanier House, "Grasslands". *c.1794. Bluegrass Pike. A single pen log structure with log additions, sided with weatherboarding and having a pegged shingle roof. This house was built on land originally part of the Fields land grant. In the first half of the twentieth century, it was operated as saddle-bred horse farm by Ike Lanier, and was the home of champion "Kalarama Colonel". NRS*

At left and below: *First Catholic Church - Fales Home.* *c.1810. N. Fifth Street, Danville. St. Patrick's Church was built about 1810 on Fifth Street, then called Chapel Street. Father Badin, the first Catholic priest ordained in America, dedicated this first brick and oldest Catholic church building in Kentucky. It had served as a Presbyterian manse and residence of the Professor Fales family by the turn of the century. The architecture changed to the Gothic Revival style around the mid 1800's. NRHD*

Batterton – Rochester House. c.1832. W. Broadway, Danville. In 1836, Mrs. Sarah Rochester deeded her mansion, Mount Airy, on East Main, to her son, moved here and lived for 10 years. The Federal style house with the later porch and dormer additions has housed apartments for many years. NRHD

Chapter III

Antebellum, 1821-1864

At the close of the settlement period and in the decades before the War Between the States, there was a slow transition from the lightness of the Federal to the sturdy boldness of the Greek Revival Style. The new construction was timber frame and brick, and included alteration and enlarging of existing settlement era dwellings. Greek-type pediments and porches were added to all manner of earlier houses, updating them, but making it difficult to place them firmly in either historical period. Both the amount and type of construction at this time is indicative of the quality of the craftsmanship available and the prosperity of the primarily agrarian economy.

Elements of the period include wide entryways with transom and sidelights, gabled front pediments, large windows, gabled or hipped low-pitched roofs, and heavily colonnaded porches with Greek or Roman capitals.

Early in the Antebellum Period, the Russel family began to introduce the fashionable new Greek inspired design to the area. They produced the brick themselves and were instrumental in the evolution of building and construction in Danville and Boyle County.

Robert Russel Sr., emigrated from Edinburgh to the United States in 1781. By the 1790's he had made his way to central Kentucky and in 1792 a son, Robert Jr., was born in Danville. Robert Jr. inherited his father's active construction business and became one of the county's leading builders and masons. His son, E.B. Russel, continued in the brick-making business beyond his father's death in 1873. The Russels have been immortalized in local history as having "found Danville made of log and left it made of brick."

Greek Revival buildings attributed to Robert Russel Jr. are two-story brick with massive porticos supported by huge plaster covered brick columns and are identified in the photo exhibit as Russel-built homes.

In 1836, development in Danville expanded to the west side of North Third Street. Dr. John Todd sold three lots to Robert Montgomery, a land promoter and developer who was active during the 1830's and 1840's. Montgomery constructed three houses between 1837 and 1842, on North Third Street in an area known as "Beaten Biscuit Row" because the sound of the biscuit beater filled the neighborhood at certain times of the day. Three of the four houses are almost identical and represent a mid-19th century upper middle class residential development, which has retained most of its original appearance.

The Gothic Revival style began in England and made its way to Central Kentucky about the middle of the 19th century. The movement sought inspiration from medieval cathedrals as well as from castles, manors and cottages. These residences are clearly discernible with their steep multi-gabled roofs, heavily ornamented chimneys, wide and deep verandas, over-hanging eaves, narrow windows (often including diamond-panels and colored glass), and fancy exterior trim commonly called "gingerbread."

The primary Gothic Revival examples in the county are thought to have been designed by Lexington architect John McMurtry, and built by Robert Russel Jr. They are known as the three "Gothic Villas," all built within a three mile radius of Danville between 1852 and 1856.

Rice – Worthington House. c.1808. Buster Pike. Reverend David Rice migrated from Virginia to Kentucky and opened Transylvania Seminary in 1785 in a three-room log cabin. Ten years later the school was moved to Lexington, becoming Transylvania University. In 1803, Edward Worthington, a judge in Mercer County and organizer of Trinity Episcopal Church, began construction on a two story Federal style house south of Rice's log cabin. In 1833, John McClain transformed the Federal structure into an updated Greek Revival timber framed dwelling with a two story recessed portico. NRL

Spears-Craig House. *c.1836. KY 33 N. A brick Federal residence with Greek Revival porch supported by Corinthian columns. NRL*

Durham House. c.1827. US 150 W. This site, first a log cabin and then this brick and frame house, has long been home to the family and descendants of John Durham. Reverend Francis Clark and Durham organized the first Methodist Society in present-day Kentucky and the church expanded westward from this location. NRS

Montgomery – Rodes House. c.1837. *North Third Street, Danville. One of three homes built by Robert Montgomery. Constructed in 1837 and lived in by the builder until 1848, when the house passed to the Clifton Rodes family. The fifth generation of that family still resides here. NRL/NRHD*

Pine Grove. c.1842. *Old Wilderness Road. This Greek Revival residence was built in 1842 by Captain Alexander McGrorty, and sat at the corner of Main and Wilderness Road. Has long been converted to apartments.*

Dr. William Pawling House. c.1847. *West Broadway. Two story Greek Revival, with one story Victorian porch added in the late 1800's. This house was one of four structures to survive the fire of 1860 which virtually destroyed downtown Danville. NRL/NRHD*
At right: *Logan Caldwell House.* c.1858. *KY 34 W. This Greek Revival home was constructed in 1858 by Logan Caldwell near the original station established by his father, James. Was long occupied in the twentieth century by the Irvin family, descendants of nearby Irvin Station. The Logans and Irvins came in the 1780's from Virginia and claimed land grants from the Revolutionary War. NRL*

Clemens Caldwell House. *c.1800-1850. North Maple Avenue at Harrodsburg Road. Seven generations of Caldwells have lived in this 200 year old home. It had its beginning as a log cabin, Betsy Clemen's dowry from her father, Jeremiah. The double inset portico with large columns was added mid-eighteenth century when the front was moved from the north to the east side.*

Smith – Jackson Funeral Home. *c.1816. Bate Street, Danville. Was originally a Federal structure built by Richard Crutchfield. A Greek portico was added later. The home has been used as a military hospital, as home of the Danville Federation of Women's clubs, and as the Banneker Elks Lodge. It has been the Smith – Jackson Funeral Home since 1958.*

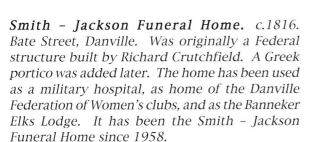

Phillip Yeiser House. *Lexington Avenue, Danville. This 1920's photo shows the original center portion of the house built in 1804 with the Greek Revival porch and wings added in the 1830's by Robert Russel, Jr. Yeiser came here in the 1790's, ran a tanning business, and built other homes in the area for his children. NRL/NRHD*

At right: *S. Harmon House.* c.1850. Second Street, Perryville. Greek Revival two story, five bay frame house with interior brick chimney, a one story porch with stout square posts over the three center bays, and entrance with transom and side lights. NRL
Below: *Bass House.* c.1843. West Lexington, Danville. A five bay, pedimented Greek Revival frame home constructed by Robert Bass, a builder who sold it in 1843 to Edward Wallis. NRHD

Above: *Bowman – Letcher House.* c.1850. East Lexington Avenue, Danville. Five bay stucco with exterior chimneys and front pediment. Believed to have been built as a wedding gift for one of the Yeiser daughters. NRL/NRHD
At left: *James Robinson House.* c.1850. North Bragg Street, Perryville. A two story, two bay frame house with one story porch. NRL

Above: *Home on East Lexington, Danville. A two story, five bay brick Greek Revival with one story porch. NRHD*

At left: *Dr. Crane House.* *c.1850. Buell Street, Perryville. 1 1/2 story, three bay brick structure with its gable end to the street and a porch supported by columns on brick piers. Served as Dr. Crane's home and office. NRL*

At right:*Burton – Polk House.* *c.1845. Buell Street, Perryville. A 1 1/2 story, four bay, asymmetrical frame house. Dr. J.J. Polk, who bought the house in 1850, treated the wounded after the Battle of Perryville. NRL*

Below:*Doram – Sledd House.* *c.1845. Martin Luther King Boulevard, Danville. This ten room frame home was built in 1845 by Doram, an indentured slave and occupied by his family until 1929. The Spillman – Sled family lived there from 1929-1991 making it perhaps the oldest continuously occupied African-American home in Danville.*

THESE RESIDENCES IN PERRYVILLE ARE ALL TWO STORY, FIVE BAY, GREEK REVIVAL EXAMPLES WITH INTERIOR CHIMNEYS. ALL HAVE CENTER HALLS AND WEATHERBOARD EXTERIORS.

Camp House. c.1845. Buell Street, Perryville. NRL

J.M. Gray House. c.1840. Bragg Street, Perryville. NRL

Addison Parks House. c. 1855. Fourth Street, Perryville. NRL

H. Hart House. c.1845. Buell Street, Perryville. NRL

At left: *Hardin – Brinton House.* c.1840. First Street, Perryville. One of the most imposing structures in Perryville, situated on a hill with a commanding view of the Chaplin River. It is a six bay, two story frame house with exterior brick end chimneys and a recessed double gallery. NRL

Below: *Bowling-Caldwell-Burton-Kern House.* c.1853 Buell Street, Perryville. This is a two story, five bay frame Greek Revival house with two story ell and double porticoes supported on square paired posts. An excellent example. NRL

Above: *Burton-Robinson House.* c.1842. Buell Street, Perryville. This home is very much like the one above, but with three bays and 1 1/2 story ell on the back. They both have large exterior end chimneys and second floor doors opening onto the porticoes. NRL

At right: *Ashhurst.* c.1848. Bluegrass Pike. This five bay, two story Greek Revival house was built in 1848 by a Mr. Clark. In 1865, Reverend Maury opened a "day school" here for young women of the Danville area. NRS

Dye House. *c.1800. Old Mackville Road. A frame over log structure with Greek Revival updating. During the Battle of Perryville, the house was used as Confederate General Simon B. Buckner's headquarters and as a hospital for injured soldiers.*

Wingate – Harberson House. *c.1850. Third Street, Perryville. A three bay, two story frame house on stone foundation, showing a large pedimented portico with second floor balcony. This imposing Greek Revival house with gable end toward the street, is the only one of its kind in Perryville. NRL*

J.B.H. Lattimore House. *c. 1850. Bragg Street, Perryville. This is a transitional two story framed dwelling with a low central gable in the five bay facade. The gable ends are bracketed and the wrap-around porch is supported by stout columns. The home was used as a hospital during the Battle of Perryville, and shows an inscription written on the wall by a soldier. NRL*

Jim Ike Harmon House. *c.1875. Crain School Road. A two story, three bay home with center hall on a stone foundation. Timber frame construction with weatherboarding. NRS*

Dr. G. B. Calvert House. *c.1855. Buell Street, Perryville. One of the few asymmetrical, "L" plan, Greek Revival Houses in Perryville. A shelf molding and simple brackets cover an entrance door with side lights and transom. NRL*

Shield – Polk House. *c.1850. Bragg Street, Perryville. This frame house with asymmetrical facade was owned by Dr. Polk, popular nineteenth century physician and surgeon. The house was damaged by artillery fire during the Battle of Perryville and has been altered. NRL*

Dr. Figg House. *c.1858. Second Street, Perryville. A two story, five bay frame Greek Revival residence with interior brick chimneys and one story porch. This house was the residence of Dr. S.N. Figg who was Dr. Polk's partner in the mid nineteenth century. It is now occupied by the Wilder Funeral Home. NRL*

James P. Mitchell House and Farmstead, *located on KY 34 in Mitchellsburg, was constructed in 1855 by Mitchell who was a prosperous farmer, businessman, and politician. He was also the owner and operator of a steam mill in Mitchellsburg, organizer of the Deposit Bank of Danville, and Postmaster in Mitchellsburg in the 1860's. This large uncommon, two story, center passage, wood-frame residence, has a dry stone foundation, hip roof with a gabled front pediment and central front porch with turned wood posts, sawn brackets and a spindle frieze. Local farmhouse venacular with Gothic Revival porch. NRL*

J.M. Wallace House. *c.1835. South Fourth Street, Danville. Recently razed. Built and lived in by Robert Russel, Jr. Unusual inset porches either side of a two story central pediment.*

Bower House. *KY 34 W. Three bay, two story frame Gothic Revival house with one story porch. NRL*

J.C. Randolf House. *c.1860. West Lexington Avenue, Danville. A five bay, two story frame home with two brick end chimneys and one story Gothic Revival porch. NRL/NRHD*

Clockwise from top left: *Bridges – Fox House.* c.1839. Maple Avenue, Danville. Built by Robert Russel, Jr. for John L. Bridges. Was also the home of Circuit Judge Fontaine T. Fox. NRL/NRHD

McFerron – Rue House. c.1822. US 127 S. Two story, three bay with classical two story portico supported by Ionic columns. The unusual central hall has an unobtrusive stairway behind the back wall. W.M. Rue, Sr. raised five-gaited saddle horses on the farm and trained them at the Danville Fairgrounds on Perryville Road at the turn of the century. NRL

"Maplewood," home of George F. Anderson, was another example of the elegant homes which once lined South Fourth Street.

James G. Birney House. "Woodlawn", c.1800. Perryville Road, Danville. Home of James G. Birney, an early Danville leader and merchant. Federal with Classical Revival additions. Wings added in 1840. Portico added 1906. This was the boyhood home of James G. Birney, son of the builder and abolitionist candidate for President. NRL

James Wilson House.
Wilson's Station, "Cragfont".
c.1785. KY 34. It faced south,
towards the Old Wilderness
Road and was one of the
earliest stations. NRL

Crow-Barbee House,
"Old Crow". c.1784.
Built by John Crow and
expanded by Thomas and
Joshua Barbee, this is
thought to be the first
stone house built west of
the Alleghenies. NRL

Philip Yeiser House. *c.1804. Lexington Avenue, Danville. Built by Robert Russel, Jr., this unusual arrangement has the large portico completely covering the 1 1/2 story facade. NRL/ NRHD*

Bryant-Slaughter House. *"Granite Hill" c.1810. KY 52 E. Granite Hill is partially a mid-nineteenth century Greek Revival, center hall plan which incorporates a portion of a very early brick dwelling which is now the rear ell. It originally faced toward the Old Wilderness Road. About 1850, a two story, brick addition with Greek revival elements including a low pitched gable roof and a symmetrical front facade was constructed. A one story, one room, kitchen wing extends to the east. NRL*

At left: *Grayson's Tavern.*
C.1785. Walnut Street, Danville.
The tavern was built by
Benjamin Grayson and was a
popular gathering place for
those who attended the
constitutional conventions and
the Danville Political Club that
was formed in 1786 by leading
men of the area. This two story
ell shaped wood frame building,
had both front and side
entrances. NRL/NRHD

Below: *Dr. Ephraim*
McDowell House. *c.1804.*
South Second Street, Danville.
Five bay, timber frame, Federal
home with an earlier brick
kitchen structure on the back.
Attached Apothecary Shoppe,
c.1790's. NRL/NRHD

Watts-Bell House. *c.1816. Constitution Square, Danville. Built by William Watts, this two story brick residence is part of Fisher Row. It was later purchased by David Bell, a leading Danville merchant. It was at Bell's house that the first meeting of the Danville Literary and Social Club was held in 1839. NRL/NRHD*

Fisher's Row Houses. *c.1817. Constitution Square. Located on the northeast of the square, they consist of two, two story brick structures on stone foundations. They were built by Jeremiah Fisher as rental property and were popular residences at that time. NRL/NRHD*

Robert Walker House. *c.1832. Located off road on a farm near the Perryville Battlefield. It is a three bay, one story Federal brick dwelling with interior chimneys, and a one story porch over the center bay. It is fronted by a stone fence with several millstones inset for ornamentation. It played an important role in the Battle of Perryville.*

Harlan-Bruce House.
C.1815. Chrisman Lane.
Built by George Harlan. A
1 1/2 story, five bay brick
structure with interior
chimneys, all on a stone
foundation. NRL

Judge John Boyle House. c.1815. Sits at a distance north of
Faulkner Lane. This simple Federal home has a central entry
highlighted by a projecting entry portico supported by plain square
columns. It is characterized by its Flemish bond brick work, raised
brick arches over each window, a stone foundation and two brick
chimneys. Judge Boyle was a political leader and U.S. Judge for
whom Boyle County was named in 1842. NRL

Ayres-Weisiger House. c.1833. West Broadway, Danville. Built
by Dr. David Ayres on land purchased from Daniel McIlvoy. The
home has a two story center section with one story flanking wings.
Around 1870, the Weisiger family renovated the home in the new
Victorian style but at this time it looks much as it did originally.
NRL/NRHD

Todd-Cheek House. *c.1836. North Third Street, Danville. This five bay, two story brick residence with the front facade laid in Flemish bond, was built by Dr. John Todd, a relative of Mary Todd Lincoln. Dr. Todd practiced medicine in Danville for many years and served as a member of the Board of Trustees for Centre College from 1833 to 1841 and from 1844 through 1847. The Greek Revival porch was added to the house when it was renovated in the mid-1800's. In 1850, the house was purchased by Dr. Alexander Robertson McKee. Dr. McKee was the son of Samuel McKee, a member of Congress from 1808 until 1816 and a member of the State Legislature and Judge of the Circuit Court. NRL/NRHD*

Proctor Rowland House. *c.1835. North Third Street, Danville. This is a five bay, two story brick structure with a one story porch supported by four small square columns. NRL/NRHD*

Above: *Montgomery-Rodes House.* c.1837. North Third Street, Danville. A two story brick structure that is only one room deep. Flemish bond brickwork enhances the front facade. A one story porch, supported by large Ionic columns, frames the main double entry doors highlighted by a transom and sidelights. The residence was built by Robert Montgomery who began construction shortly after purchasing the land from Dr. Todd. Montgomery resided there until 1848 when he sold the property to Clifton Rodes, Governor Owsley's son-in-law, whose father was one of the earliest settlers of Kentucky. NRL/NRHD

At right: *Bowman-Anderson House.* C.1842. North Third Street, Danville. This five bay, two story stuccoed structure has four pairs of columns supporting the porch that extends along the entire front. This home was built by Robert Montgomery. NRL/NRHD

Old Centre. C.1820. Centre College Campus, Danville. Centre College was chartered by the Kentucky Legislature on January 1, 1819. Old Centre was built in 1820 in the Georgian Revival style and is perhaps the oldest college building west of the Allegheny Mountains. It was later updated, adding a wing on each side of the main block and a giant portico over the main entry, thereby giving a classical order temple front to a relatively sedate structure. *NRL*

Karrick-Parks House. c.1856. Buell Street, Perryville. A Federal style, two story brick home with five bays. In the back yard is a cave that was used by early settlers as an underground passage for escaping Indians. During the Battle of Perryville the house and dependencies were used for officers quarters and it is said the soldiers "drank the cave dry". After the war, reportedly a croquet game was kept continuously going in the back yard for over 50 years. *NRL*

Crawford House. c.1840. US 68 E. The Crawford house is a brick structure with a stone foundation, a large central chimney near the rear and smaller ones in the gable ends of the wings. It seems to represent a transition between the Federal and Greek Revival styles. The most unusual feature is the recessed porch under the central upper story. The house is located on the route taken by the Confederate army as they approached Perryville from Harrodsburg, and served as General Bragg's headquarters during the Battle. *NRL*

"Roselawn".   Governor William Owsley House. c.1848. US 127 N. This is a five bay "L" plan home with center hall and large portico typical of the Greek Revival style. The Ionic columns were the trademark of builder Robert Russel, Jr., who built this home for the retirement of Congressman and Governor Owsley. NRL

Elmwood Academy. c.1850. Fourth Street, Perryville. This is a five bay, two story building with center hall and tall pedimented portico and balcony. It was used as a hospital during the Battle of Perryville, a residence until 1891, and a school from 1892 to 1925, when it again became a residence. It has in recent years also been used as an inn and tea room. NRL

W.H. Haskins House. c.1850. Lexington Road, Danville. Built by the Talbots, a three bay frame home with center gable and heavily ornamented one story portico. Danville's best example of Carpenter Gothic. NRL

Situated on US 127, one mile north of Danville. It was built between 1852 and 1854 for Thomas and Joseph Helm. NRL

Located three miles south of Danville on US 127 S., was built in 1856 by John Fouche Warren and Samuel Warren. NRL

Although many of Boyle County's architecturally significant antebellum residences display traditional three and five bay front facades beneath low gabled and hipped roofs, there are a surprising number of Victorian Gothic residences located in the immediate vicinity. Three Gothic villas constructed between 1852 and 1856 within three miles of Danville are the Helm-Gentry House, Mound Cottage, and Warrenwood. All are of brick masonry construction and were built by established and prosperous Boyle County families on large tracts of farmland. These center passage floor plans display interior woodwork that is essentially Greek Revival. The design of these three houses is attributed to Lexington architect John McMurtry (1812-1890), master of the Gothic Revival style, and Danville native, Robert Russel, Jr. who constructed these traditionally planned and detailed homes.

Maple Avenue, Danville, is most elaborate of the three Danville Gothic houses and is a superb example of the Gothic Revival style. The residence was built in 1856 for Jeremiah Tilford Boyle, son of Judge John Boyle, the namesake of Boyle County. J.T. Boyle was a lawyer and well known Union Officer during the War. NRL

At left: *"Spring Hill." Thomas Lillard House.* *c.1855. US 150 E.* This is a three bay brick residence with a center hall. It is primarily in the Greek Revival style but shows Italianate influences indicating the transition between the periods. Thomas M. and Mary Bright Lillard came to Kentucky from Virginia around 1848, eventually acquiring 600 acres on the old Wilderness Road. The farm served as a camp for Union soldiers during the War, and stayed in the Lillard family until the early twentieth century. *NRL*

Below: *Boyle County Court House.* After the disastrous fire of 1860, the third courthouse, a Christopher Wren-like structure, was constructed by James R. Carrigan. It became a Union hospital after the Battle of Perryville in October 1862, and repairs were necessary before the courts could reconvene. *NRL*

Charles T. Worthington House. c.1855. Bluegrass Pike. An Italianate example, "L" plan, with center hall. It has a hipped roof, bracketed eaves, paired tall narrow windows, and took six years to complete due to the degree of ornamentation. *NRL*

At right: *Cambus Kenneth Estate.* *c.1885. US 127 By-pass. This impressive residence was built on the site of a previous house that was built circa 1790 by famous pioneer surgeon, Dr. Ephraim McDowell, who used it for his family's summer retreat. The estate was named Cambus Kenneth by Dr. McDowell for the ruins of the Abbey of Cambuskenneth in Sterling, Scotland. A later owner, James G. Cecil, a wealthy merchant, farmer, stock trader, and his son, Charles P. Cecil, built the present Italianate style residence. It was designed by James G. Cecil's wife who based the plans on a family house in Columbia, Tennessee. Charles P. Cecil with brother, Granville raised saddlebred horses and operated a racetrack on Second street near Clark's Run in the early 1900's. Granville Cecil became the first President of Farmers National Bank in 1879 and was the grandfather of Cecil Dulin Wallace to whom this book is dedicated. NRL*

T. McRoberts House. *c.1875. West Broadway, Danville. This house was built by former Minnesota State Senator Thomas McRoberts and his bride, Mary Louise. NRL/NRHD*

Jacob's Hall. c.1855. South Second Street, Danville. This is the oldest surviving building on the campus of the Kentucky School for the Deaf. The site, adjacent to the school's first ten acre tract, was owned by J.A. Jacobs, then superintendent of the institution and the man for whom the building was named. Designed by architect Thomas Lewinski and built by John McMurtry, construction began in 1855 and was completed two years later. This four story brick Italianate building housed all the school's major functions until 1882. It has a one story entrance portico that is supported by brick piers. A horizontal band of stone wraps around the building dividing the first and second floors. Carved wood brackets accent the roof line making this one of the most notable Italianate buildings in Boyle County. NRL

Frazer House. *c.1880. West Broadway. Built by the Wiseman family in the Queen Anne style with gables, turret, and wrap-around porch. NRL/NRHD*

Boyle Rodes House. *c.1910. East Lexington Avenue, Danville. A one story porch with central pediment spans the facade of this two story wood frame, central passage residence reflecting the Colonial Revival style. NRL/NRHD*

At left: *c. 1800. This house on East Main is a frame 1 1/2 story structure with steeply gabled dormers, was built at the end of the Queen Anne period and exhibits elements of the Classical Revival style. NRHD*

Federal Building. c.1910. West Main Street, Danville. This two story stone building was originally constructed as a Post Office. It is typical in style and materials of other post office buildings in Kentucky and is in the Beaux Arts style. NRL

Carnegie Library. c.1913. Centre College Campus. This Classical Revival structure was originally designed as a library for Central University and has been used also as an admissions office, book store and post office. It is a five bay, two story building with a mansard tile roof and bracketed eaves. Arched and rectangular windows are capped with stone. NRL

Boyle County Public Library. c.1937. North Third Street, Danville. The Danville Public Library began as a subscription library in 1893 and opened in a Main Street drugstore with 100 members and 300 books. After several relocations, the library was situated on North Third Street at Broadway. It was designed in the Georgian Revival style by architect Charles Celarius of Cincinnati and built by John W. Wood of Danville, after a generous bequeath from Eugenia and Sarah Young, daughters of Centre College President John C. Young. NRL

Union Monument. Perryville Battlefield. NRL

Confederate Monument. Perryville Battlefield. NRL

Confederate Monument. McDowell Park, West Main Street, Danville. NRL

The only monument ever erected by the Union for Confederate dead. Goodnight Cemetery, Claunch Road. NRL

Fackler House. *Was on the east side of Lebanon Road near present industrial area, and was the home of Calvin Fackler's parents. Fackler wrote our first history, Early Days in Danville.*

Rochester-Farris Mansion. "Mount Airy". c.1832. *East Main Street, Danville. This 40 room mansion, built by Robert Russel, Jr., sat on a hill overlooking the Old Wilderness Road. It was razed in 1957 to make way for Jennie Rogers School.*

Above: *C.C.Moore House and farm. "Blythewood"* c.1852. *US 127 N. A five bay Greek Revival example with center hall and monumental portico. Built by Robert Russel, Jr. NRL*

At left: *McClure-Barbee House.* c.1845. *South Fourth Street, Danville. Built by Robert Russel, Jr. for Samuel P. Barbee and long the home of the McClure family. Greek Revival style mansion with unusual inset portico, supported by two massive pillars. NRL*

Fisher-Byington House. *c.1845. South Fourth Street, Danville. Built by Robert Russel, Jr.*

Peter Mason House. *c.1820. US 127 N. Was originally a two story, five bay, center hall Federal. The Greek Revival portico added in 1950. Built by Robert Russel, Jr. and sited on a 1500 acre tract. NRL*

Christian Gore House. *c.1859. Proctor Street, Danville. Built by Robert Russel, Jr. for Christian Gore. A seven bay, brick dwelling with center portico supported by large but simple columns, with a pedimented entrance. Home of the Danville Board of Education. NRL*

Sandifor House. *c.1848. East Lexington Avenue, Danville. This Greek Revival home was built by Robert Russel, Jr. for a Yeiser daughter. It has a raised center section flanked by two story wings with balustrade and is an unusual type in Danville. NRL/NRHD*

Rochester-Cecil House. "Melrose" *c.1854. An "L" plan with center hall and one story ionic portico. This Greek Revival home was built by Charles Rochester and purchased in 1878 by Granville Cecil. Cecil, owner of a racetrack with his brother Charles, was an early leader of the saddlebred horse industry. NRL*

P. Engleman House. "Cecilhurst". *McDowell Drive, Danville. A Greek Revival residence, early section dating to 1821. Originally built by the Fisher family of Fisher's Garrison.*

At left: *J.S. Wallace House.* *c.1850.* *KY 33 N. This appealing 1 1/2 story Gothic Revival home has bracketed eaves, board and batten siding, joined chimney stacks, and colored glass windows. NRL*

Above left: Hunter House. *c.1870. US 127 N. This structure is on the property of the Peter Mason home and was probably a tenant dwelling. It has the Gothic detailing and gingerbread trim common in this period. NRS*

Above right: T.W. Bottom House. *c.1855. Third Street, Perryville. A two story, three bay frame on a stone foundation with interior brick chimneys and three frontal gables. The style is simplified Gothic. NRL*

At left: Brinton House. *c.1855. First Street, Perryville. This home is simplified Gothic but with multiple dormers and a porch on two sides. It is a two story, three bay with narrow paired windows. NRL*

Dr. Wallace Green House. *c.1855. Bragg Street, Perryville. This house was the home of Dr. Green, a prominent physician and druggist. It is highly ornamented Gothic Revival in style. It sits on a lovely site, and includes this dependency with shaped roof and spike. NRL*

Left: **Hutchings House.** *c.1855. KY 52 E. at Hubble Road. Attractive Gothic Revival, two story wood frame with elaborate detailing.*

Below: *Frame House.* *East Lexington Avenue, Danville. With tri-gable facade, paired windows, and paired interior chimneys. Gothic Revival. NRHD*

At right: *Briscoe White House.* c.1850. Buell Street, Perryville. *This is a 1 1/2 story, five bay brick with a Gothic inspired center gable and an asymmetrical window arrangement. Mr. White was a prominent banker and the bank is directly to the north.* NRL

Below:*G.W. Doneghy House.* c.1800. West Lexington Avenue, Danville. *A wonderful three bay, Gothic Revival cottage with a log center section and two interior brick chimneys. This is one of the earliest structures remaining on the street. The unusual shiplap siding, three front gables, and Gothic trim were added to the dogtrot form around 1840.* NRL/NRHD

Terhune House. Built and altered 1820-1855. First Street, Perryville. This is a primitive federal cottage with Gothic additions, including center gable and gingerbread.NRL

Benjamin Perkins House. c.1818. North Second Street, Danville. *This early house has seen several changes, including the three Gothic Revival ornamented gables. It was a very simply styled Federal form, judging from its original date. Mr. Perkins, about 1800, owned and operated an inn and stage coach stop and the Danville Brewery.* NRL/NRHD

Helm-Gentry House. *c.1852. US 127 N. Built for Thomas and Joseph Helm and sold to the Gentry family in the 1870's.NRL*

Mound Cottage. *c.1856. Maple Avenue, Danville. A Gothic Revival home with three gables and ornamented porch. NRL*

R.L.Salter House. *c.1870. Dogwood Dr. Victorian home with a tri-gabled tower on the east side. NRS*

CHAPTER IV

Post Bellum, 1865-1899

During the War Between the States, construction virtually halted. Boyle County was not subjected to wide spread pillage and fire during the conflict, but many buildings, both public and private, were used during the Battle of Perryville, mostly for tending the sick and wounded. There are many anecdotal stories of bloodied floors and stains that could never be removed.

In spite of post-war depression and reconstruction, and largely due to rail expansion, building slowly resumed, beginning an architectural period known as Victorian. It included several styles, some of them quite exuberant in detail.

The immediate emphasis was on a new style, actually introduced shortly before the war, and taking inspiration from the Mediterranean farmhouse. The Italianate home was exhibited in two types. A box shape with perfectly balanced symmetry was known as "Tuscan Revival." The "Italian Villa" was asymmetrical and usually shaped in an "L". Typical to the Italianate were a low-hipped roof, wide bracketed overhangs and narrow clustered windows which sometimes formed a bay.

In both urban and rural areas of the county other dwellings reveal the influence of the Queen Anne style, a term that is particularly synonymous with the Victorian Era. It is characterized by steep gables, high chimneys and intricate detailing. Building materials run the gamut from board and batten to a rich mixture of wood, brick and stone. Several other styles appear to a lesser extent locally and primarily in the urban setting.

Second Empire typically included a mansard roof with a bracketed cornice and iron cresting. Romanesque buildings are very ornamental, sometimes using various colors and textures of stone laid in bands or arches, ornamental brick corbelling and roofs of tile.

A style used extensively in the area is one that might be termed Folk Victorian. Railroads made available to local lumber yards pre-cut and very detailed, and inexpensive trim designs. Many builders simply grafted these new pieces onto traditional farm house forms, updating these simple structures with new Victorian porches and trim.

T.McRoberts House. *c.1875. West Broadway, Danville. This two story brick T-plan residence, built between 1875 and 1877, has hood molds above the openings, paired brackets along the eaves, and a one story cast iron porch. An excellent example of the Italianate form. NRL/NRHD*

Curry House. *c.1880. Lexington Avenue, Danville. Built by J.A. Curry in the Queen Anne style with highly stylized wrap-around porches, removed in the 1970's. NRHD*

J. Pope House. *KY 52. A Greek Revival frame residence with stone foundation and exterior chimneys and later porch. NRS*

Cheek House. *West Main Street, Danville. A frame Italianate with double bay windows and bracketed window hoods. NRS*

Harlan-Robinson House. *c.1872. KY 52. Italianate, three bay, two story dwelling with bay window and a later Classical Revival porch. NRS*

Samuel Ewing House. *Buell Street, Perryville. Built in the mid-nineteenth century. This is a frame dwelling, two bay, two story with center chimney. NRL*

House on South Third Street, Danville. Gothic Revival, L-plan, brick over stone foundation with interior chimneys and wonderful porch. NRS

Minor House. "Lynnwood" KY 34 W. Began about 1830 as a log house facing north, to which a simple Federal style structure was added about 1845, by J.B. Speed, moving the entrance to the south facade. Later improvements including the massive portico with exuberant detailing were added in 1910 by the Shuttleworths, bringing the structure clearly into the Chateausque style of the times. In 1917, the Minor family purchased the property, which included the landmark Clock Barn. The home burned in 1977 and the barn was razed in 1996.

Willis Grimes House. *c.1860. KY 34 W. A two story brick, three bay Italianate vernacular house with hipped roof, bay window, double bracketed eaves. NRL*

Nimrod Buster House and Farmstead. *c.1876. Buster Pike. The Nimrod I. Buster House and farmstead is a two story Italianate brick residence. It has two major facades, one symmetrical and one asymmetrical, a low intersecting gabled roof with wide eaves and brackets, and narrow windows. Buster, a native of Wayne County, was an accomplished farmer. NRL*

J.D.Goodloe House. *c.1860. West Broadway, Danville. Built by attorney John Goodloe, it is a three bay, T-plan structure with a bay window in a front gable facade. It has double and triple brackets, hooded windows, and a one story porch. NRHD*

Moore-Welsh House. *c.1859. West Main Street, Danville. Has been home to the Centre College presidents since 1937. Built by William Moore in the Italianate style, it is a two story brick home with early twentieth century Classical Revival porch. NRL*

Preston and Prewitt Funeral Home. *South Fourth Street, Danville. This large Italianate structure was built as a dwelling in the third quarter of the nineteenth century.*

J.W. Proctor House. *c.1870. North Third Street, Danville. Two story Italianate townhouse, unusual for Danville, sits adjacent to the street with a recessed side passage. NRL/NRHD*

J.T. Curry House. *W. Lexington Avenue, Danville. A three bay, two story home in the Italianate style with more recent tall Classical Revival porch. NRHD*

Guthrie-May-Raley House. *c.1813. KY 243. A three bay brick dwelling, was originally a two bay, hall parlor plan house with asymmetrical entry. The third bay was added in the late nineteenth century. Believed to be the oldest brick house in the Rolling Fork area. NRL*

Sallee House. *c.1824. North Third Street, Danville. An early brick town house, remodeled in the Italianate style in 1850. Two story, three bay with inset asymmetrical entry. NRL/NRHD*

House on Old Lexington Rd., *Danville. c.1890. Stucco over frame with projecting bay window and arched hood moldings.*

L.B. Ralston House. *Waterworks Road. Probably an Italianate example with Colonial Revival influenced additions, including a two story portico supported by large square columns. NRS*

Gentry House. *c.1890. US 150 E. A frame Italianate example with Colonial Revival porch added in 1917. NRL*

James Robinson house and farm. *c.1900. KY 1856 near Mitchellsburg. This thirteen room house is one of the few Queen Anne residences in the county. This 1 1/2 story wood-frame center hall dwelling covered with weatherboarding and shingle siding, has a hipped roof with several projecting gables, and a central turret. NRS*

House on Webster Road. *This is a home showing styles in transition, and includes a bracketed center gable, paired windows, two center chimneys and a Gothic Revival porch.*

Crain – McGraw House *on Short Line Road. A frame, two story, three bay home with pierced center gable and Victorian porch. NRS*

Isaacs House and Farmstead. *Rawlings Road near Gravel Switch. Two story frame farmhouse. NRL*

Kate Park House. *c.1870. Buell Street, Perryville. 1 1/2 story frame on stone foundation. It is a Victorian cottage with rounded dormer and gingerbread porch. One of a kind in Perryville. NRL*

Methodist Parsonage. *Second Street, Perryville. A small two story, three bay house with asymmetrical entry, hipped roof, and gabled bay window over the door. NRS*

House on Second Street, *Perryville. A frame, two story, three bay, "L" plan. NRS*

Jacob Cozatt House. *c.1870. Parksville. This two story frame dwelling is believed to be the oldest residence in Parksville. Five generations of the family have owned the home. NRS*

G.T. Helm residence. *Corner of Broadway and Second Street, Danville. A Folk Victorian cottage in a bucolic setting downtown. Razed.*

T.B. Bright House and Farmstead. *c.1794. KY 34 E. A very early log house encased in a two story, five bay frame with ornamented low center gable and Victorian wrap-around porch. NRL*

J.S. and Nannie Vanarsdale House. *c.1881. US 150 W at Atoka. This simple two story, T-plan house was ornamented in the late nineteenth century with bracketed eaves, Victorian porch frieze and shaped lintels. NRL*

Rust House. c.1898. West Lexington Ave. This Georgian Revival frame house with balustrade roof and porch and center dormers in all four facades is truly unique in Danville. This cubic form with hipped roof took inspiration from the late nineteenth century homes in the Northeast. NRL/NRHD

Queen Anne House. c.1895. East Lexington, Danville was built by A.C.Gibbons on land that was part of the Danville Female Academy. NRHD

At left and above: *House on West Broadway,* Danville. *Two views. A brick Queen Anne with wrap around porch. NRHD*

Below: *House on Fifth Street* at Broadway, Danville. *Queen Anne stucco with large round turret and asymmetrically placed dormer. NRHD*

John Quisenberry House. c.1890. *West Lexington Avenue, Danville. A two story brick Queen Anne with projecting wing, corbelled chimneys and segmented brick arches over the windows. The brick dependency to the west was originally the slave quarters of the Yeiser house next door. NRL/NRHD*

Robert P. Jacobs House. c.1882. *West Lexington, Danville. A picturesque and complex Queen Anne example with corbelled chimneys and asymmetrical porch. Descendants of this family were instrumental in the building of the public library in the 1930's. NRL/NRHD*

Frame Cottage. Late Victorian. East Lexington Avenue, Danville. With wrap-around porch. *NRHD*

House on West Lexington Avenue, Danville. A two story Colonial Revival example with one story porch, built at the turn of the century. *NRHD*

Two views: A 1 1/2 story folk Victorian cottage on East Lexington Avenue, Danville. *NRHD*

FOUR EXAMPLES OF LATE VICTORIAN COTTAGES

West Lexington, NRHD

West Lexington, NRHD

West Lexington, NRHD

West Lexington, NRHD

THREE, TWO STORY, FRAME QUEEN ANNE EXAMPLES WITH ONE STORY PORCHES.

East Lexington. NRHD

West Broadway. NRHD

West Broadway. NRHD

Two story, frame, Queen Anne examples, all having gabled projecting wings, bay windows, and one story porches with gingerbread trim.

West Lexington. NRHD

East Lexington. NRHD

Robertson House. *c.1890. West Lexington. NRL/NRHD*

FOUR FRAME HOMES IN THE FREE CLASSIC STYLE COMMON AFTER 1890.

East Lexington.   NRHD

West Lexington.   NRHD

Left: *West Lexington. NRHD* **Above:** *West Lexington.   NRHD*

THREE QUEEN ANNES WITH MUCH HAPPY VICTORIAN DETAILING, INCLUDING A TURRET, GABLES, AND GINGERBREAD.

North Broadway. NRHD

West Lexington. NRHD

West Lexington. NRHD

East Lexington. NRHD

East Lexington. NRHD

Baptist Church Parsonage. West Lexington. NRL/NRHD

West Lexington. NRHD

Right: *House on East Lexington, Danville. Earlier than most in the area. A five bay, two story frame with Colonial Revival porch. NRHD*

Below: *House on East Lexington Avenue, Danville. A transitional Colonial. NRHD*

Left: *Hickman Carter House. c.1910. East Lexington Avenue, Danville. Dutch Colonial with continuous frontal dormer and porch with paired columns. NRL/NRHD*

House on West Lexington with projecting bay and square asymmetrical porch. NRHD

Above: *House on North Third.* c.1910. Classical Revival. NRHD
Left: *House on East Lexington,* Classical Revival. c.1915. NRHD

Jones house. c.1900. South Fourth Street, Danville.Razed 1970.

House on West Broadway. c.1890. A frame, two story with a three bay projecting wing with bay window and elaborately detailed one story porch. NRL/NRHD

House on North Fifth Street, Danville. Two story frame, late Victorian. NRHD

A two story brick house with square tower. Walnut street, Danville. Log portion thought to be the Willis Russel house located on East Walnut today.

1925 GARDEN PARTY AT THE QUISENBERRY HOUSE. *"Longmeade" was relocated and rebuilt in 1918, on the site of the old Danville Fairgrounds on Perryville Road. NRS*

CHAPTER V

Early Modern, 1900-1945

Boyle County and the rest of the Middle South at the turn of the century moved toward residential architecture of interior and exterior forms quite different from the Victorian. The growing population desired affordable functional dwellings to fit on urban and suburban lots and to meet the spatial needs of families who rarely employed domestic help. Several factors enabled the national acceptance of new building styles. Influenced by the industrial revolution of the late 19th century, low cost, mass-produced building materials including dimensional framing lumber, sash windows, millwork, and nails enabled builders to construct a "Pattern Book" house practically anywhere materials could be delivered. Entire house kits were available from companies such as Sears and Roebuck.

Following in the footsteps of the Russel family, A.W. Walker was the prominent contractor in the early 20th century and built many handsome structures in Danville's historic districts. He came to the Junction City area in 1881 from Shipthorp, England, and is said to have been born on the ship coming over. He built homes, schools, churches and dormitories in a variety of the latest styles.

The first half of the century is commonly known as the Early Modern Period and included such varied building styles as: Classical and Colonial Revival, Tudor Revivals, Chatequesque, Beaux Arts, Prairie and Craftsman.

Colonial and Classical Revivals paired elements of earlier Federal and Greek periods with updated floor plans, in order to recapture the past and improve the interior arrangements.

The Tudor style is distinguished by half-timbering in combination with stucco, slate roofs and leaded glass windows.

Chatequesque is a relatively rare style loosely based on the country manors of France, featuring steeply pitched hipped roofs, towers, turrets, dormers, ornamental metal, arched windows and doors, and massive masonry. It could be termed a melding of Gothic and Renaissance.

Beaux Arts is a classical style with exuberant ornamentation including flat roofs, elaborate moldings, dentils, balustrades, balconies, window crowns, quoins, pilasters and columns.

Frank Lloyd Wright created the Prairie style originally in Chicago but it was widely distributed in pattern books of the time and is recognized throughout the country, including in Danville. It is characterized by a horizontal emphasis achieved through low-pitched hipped roofs, widely overhanging eaves, two stories in combination with one story porches with massive square supports. American Foursquare is a sub-type of Prairie, its earliest form and the most common local version of the style.

The Arts and Crafts movement in the early part of the 20th century inspired the design for the Craftsman house commonly known as the bungalow. Conventional forms found in Boyle County are recognized by their ground hugging appearance, angled roofs, wide eave overhangs with exposed rafter ends, central front dormers and full frontal porches supported by large square columns. Exteriors may be wood, brick, shingle, stone, stucco, or any combination thereof. Their typically 1-1/2 story interiors have few hallways and room arrangements are dictated by function rather than formality.

The majority of bungalows are located in Danville and Junction City and were built to house the growing, working family. Cottage bungalows, located in the agricultural settings, were sometimes constructed as tenant houses.

This period in architecture spans the half-century that included explosive population growth, a shift in the work force from farm to town, the automobile revolution, prosperity and depression, and two world wars. Perhaps that is why we see such diversity in the structures of this period. Examples of each can be found spread through all the historic districts in Danville and throughout the county, as the photo history will exhibit.

Top left: *House on East Lexington Avenue*, Danville. Colonial Revival. NRHD
Bottom left: *House on West Broadway*, Danville. Colonial Revival. NRHD
Above: *House on West Broadway*, Danville. Late Victorian. Stucco over frame. NRHD

Grider House on West Lexington, Danville. Frame with changes.
NRS/NRHD

House on East Lexington, Danville. Classical Revival.
NRHD

Yates - Hudson House on East Lexington, Danville. c.1900. Classical Revival. NRL/NRHD

House on West Main Street, Danville. *c.1900. Classical Revival with Chateauesque features rare in Danville.*

E.B. Russel House. c.1872. West Main Street, Danville. Built by E.B.Russel and his wife for their home. It has since been used as a residence, an Elks Club, and professional offices. A Romanesque form in red brick with terra-cotta sculpture, large central dormer, and double arched entry. Unique in Danville.

Gentry House. c.1906. East Lexington Avenue, Danville. A Colonial Revival example. Two story stucco with gables crowning the end bays. NRL/NRHD

Richardson House. c.1900. Fifth Street at Broadway, Danville. Prairie style with a broad overhanging hipped roof supported by long brackets. Completely rebuilt and remodeled in 1929 by Colonel Richardson, it was originally servant's quarters and later the Sigma Chi Fraternity house. NRL/NRHD

Above and top left: *Minor House.* c.1913. West Broadway, Danville. Colonial Revival. Early view shows open porch prior to glass enclosure. Built by A.W.Walker for R.L.Salter. NRS/NRHD
Middle left: *House.* c.1922. West Lexington Avenue. Colonial Revival built by A.W.Walker for Nelson Rodes. Sr. NRHD
Lower left: *Banks Hudson House.* c.1919. West Lexington Avenue, Danville. Classical Revival with hipped roof and wide eave overhangs, showing a transition into the Prairie style. Built by A.W.Walker. NRL/NRHD

Randolf Mock Farm. *"Cedar Grove". c.1800. Gwinn Island Road. The original log structure located here burned and this Colonial Revival brick and stone residence was built in 1924. NRL*

Charles Caldwell Residence. *c.1925. KY 34. This residence was constructed on the site of the original dwelling that was destroyed by fire in the early twentieth century. Frankel and Curtis Architects designed a popular adaptation of the common center-hall plan using Classical Revival motifs. It has smooth stone lintels above tripartite windows, dormers, a one story central entry portico, with grouped Doric columns, balcony, and a Mediterranean inspired tile roof. NRL*

Mary Simpson Oldham House. *US 150 W. This house, with restrained ornamentation, was built in 1940 after the original 1876 residence was destroyed. This two story brick residence is a fine example of the Classical Revival style, popular in the early twentieth century. This center hall dwelling has a symmetrical front facade, classical entry portico, tile roof, and one story wings, balancing the central mass. NRL*

House on East Lexington Avenue, *Danville. Brick Colonial Revival with full frontal porch. NRHD*

House on Maple Avenue, *Danville. Brick Colonial Revival with asymmetrical porch. NRHD*

House on West Lexington Avenue, *Danville. Brick American Foursquare. NRHD*

At left and above: *House on West Lexington Avenue,* Danville. *This structure was originally a dependency of the Benjamine Perkins House. In 1914 it became the Blue Bird Tea Room. Lettie and Nannie Green served sandwiches and desserts for the girls of the Kentucky College for Women, just down the street. In 1930, the Riffes added a second story and opened the Covered Wagon Antique Shop. When this business moved out to the edge of town, the building became a residence, as it is today. NRHD*

At right: *House.* c.1922. West Broadway, Danville. *Craftsman style bungalow with Tudor Revival influences. NRHD*
Below: *House.* c.1920. Adams Street, Danville. *A one story frame dwelling wonderfully sited near Old Crow.*

At left and below: *Henry Cutter Houses.* c.1930. *Junction City. Two brick bungalows located on adjacent lots in Junction City on the south side of Shelby Street, attributed to local contractor, builder and lumber mill owner, Henry Cutter. 1 1/2 story of yellow ochre glazed brick with hip roofs which extend as full-width porches, supported by square brick columns on each front facade.NRL*

Below: *House on Alta Avenue,* Danville. *Typical bungalow form with wide eve overhangs and angled roof.*

Above: *House on West Lexington,* Danville. Brick American Foursquare. *NRHD*

At right: *House on Maple,* Danville. Brick bungalow. *NRHD*

At left and above: *Houses.* *West Lexington Avenue. Danville. These two brick bungalows were built by a Mr. Robinson, for himself and his sister, after moving the old house that was on the lot to Leonard Court. c. 1930. NRHD*

Wilderness Road, Danville. Tudor Revival with dominant front gable. NRHD

Wilderness Road, Danville. Bungalow in stucco and geodes. NRHD

Lazy Acres Farm. c.1925. US 127 S. An unusual example of a bungalow. A one story, two room, hipped roof cottage with a recessed central entry. In 1935, the residence evolved into its present form as a front gabled bungalow that is 1 1/2 stories tall with stuccoed walls inset with yellowish geodes, an asphalt shingle roof, and a one bay side gable extension. The date "1935" is inscribed in small geodes across the front gabled end. NRL

House on Maple Avenue, Danville. Front gabled roof on Colonial Revival form. *NRHD*

House on Maple Avenue, Danville. Victorian vernacular. *NRL/NRHD*

House on Maple Avenue, Danville. A frame raised cottage, unusual in the area. *NRHD*

At right: *House on Maple Avenue,* Danville. c.1847. One of the first homes on the Harrodsburg Pike, this frame Greek Revival with early log sections, was moved forward on the lot in 1900 when the street became Maple Avenue and infilled with modern dwellings. NRHD

At left: *House on Maple Avenue,* Danville. c.1847. Italianate with revisions. NRHD

House on Maple Avenue, Danville. Two views: mid-nineteenth Italianate form with a later Victorian porch and trim added. *NRHD*

House on Maple Avenue, Danville. *Transitional styling including Classical Revival with prairie influence. NRHD*

At left: *Phillip-Nichols House*. *c.1890. Maple Avenue, Danville. Queen Anne with two circular towers. NRL/NRHD*
Lower left: *House on Maple Avenue*, *Danville. Urban Folk Victorian. NRHD*
Lower right: *House on Maple Avenue*, *Danville. Urban Folk Victorian. NRHD*

House on Maple Avenue, Danville. *Classical Revival. NRHD*

Above: *House on Maple Avenue,* Danville. *Classical Revival. NRHD*
At left: *William Brewer House. c.1860. Maple Avenue, Danville. Two story brick Italianate with paired bracketing and bay window. Mr. Brewer ran a livery stable downtown. NRL/NRHD*

House on Maple Avenue, Danville. Frame Urban Folk Victorian. Two story with gabled front wing. *NRHD*

House on Maple Avenue, Danville. Urban Folk Victorian. Frame two story with gabled wing. *NRHD*

House on Maple Avenue, Danville. *Queen Anne example with many alterations. NRHD*

House on Maple Avenue, Danville. Colonial Revival. NRHD

Above and at right: *House on Maple Avenue,* Danville. Before and after. NRHD

House on Maple Avenue, *Danville. c.1908. This Colonial Revival house was the Wise Guest House in the 1920's, accommodating the motoring public before motels were common. NRHD*

House on Maple Avenue, *Danville. Is a large home whose life spans decades and shows many influences, including bracketed eaves, shaped window tops, and columned one story porch. NRHD*

House on Maple Avenue, Danville. Colonial Revival. NRHD

House on Maple Avenue, Danville. Prairie Style stucco with hipped roof, recessed porch and center dormer. NRHD

Alumni House. c.1900. Maple Avenue, Danville. Classical Revival with three large dormers across the front roof, and quoins on the facade. NRL/NRHD

House on Maple Avenue, *Danville. One story bungalow of ochre brick, with hipped roof, dormer, and multiple windows. NRHD*

House on Maple Avenue, *Danville. American Foursquare, typical example. NRHD*

House on Maple Avenue, *Danville. A frame Craftsman example. NRHD*

House on Maple Avenue, Danville. *Early frame Folk Victorian bungalow with unusual porch and trim.* NRHD

House on Maple Avenue, Danville. *An unchanged example of bungalow style with unusual detailing in the dormer windows.* NRHD

House on Maple Avenue, Danville. 1 1/2 story Tudor Revival brick cottage.

House on Maple Avenue, Danville. Frame bungalow with large windows and recessed dormer.

House on Maple Avenue, Danville. Typical brick bungalow with large front dormer.

House. c.1942. Maple Avenue, Danville. Brick Colonial Revival with two story porch. NRHD

Bryant House. c.1938. KY 34 E. Brick and stone Colonial Revival with two story porch and gable fan light.

House on Maple Avenue, Danville. Frame Colonial Revival with pieced balustrade. NRHD

Charles Ridgeway House. *Old US 127 S., Junction City. A Victorian frame farm house with double interior chimneys, and central roof gable covering paired windows and highlighted with fancy Victorian trim.*

Ellis House. *c.1900. Forkland. Built by James Condor. Frame Folk Victorian. "L" plan with porch and unusual trim.*

J.J. Moore House. *c.1920. KY 34 W. This 1 1/2 story single family dwelling is an outstanding bungalow in the county. The weatherboard sided house has a low pitched roof pierced by four hip dormers. A porch which spans the front facade is supported by square wood posts. Locally found geodes decorate the central interior chimney. NRL*

House. *Frame Victorian farm house in the Forkland area.*

EAST MAIN
HISTORIC DISTRICT

The East Main Street Historic District is a group of stylistically cohesive residences which are distinguished from the other surrounding residential area. The scale, materials, and setback of these houses convey the blend of craftsmanship and technology which characterized turn-of-the-century architecture.

The eastern end of Main Street was developed as Otter's Addition in the 1890's. Built on uniformly-sized lots within a span of two decades, the houses are similar in style and materials. The first house, built in 1895, is an eclectic and symmetrical Queen Anne and is adjacent to a group of transitional Classical Revival residences.

A second group of houses have transitional features linked to both Queen Anne and Classical Revival styles. Eclectic detailing includes Palladian windows, stained glass and pedimented dormers.

Queen Anne. NRHD

Queen Anne. NRHD

At left and above: *Roberts House.*
Queen Anne. NRHD

Dunn House. *c.1903. Classical Revival. NRL/NRHD*

Queen Anne. NRHD

Queen Anne. NRHD

Queen Anne. NRHD

Reid House. *Queen Anne. NRHD*

Queen Anne. NRHD

Queen Anne. NRHD

Queen Anne. NRHD

Colonial Revival. NRHD

Victorian Vernacular. NRHD

Victorian Vernacular. NRHD

Harding House. Victorian Vernacular. NRHD

Colonial Revival. NRHD

American Foursquare. NRHD

Queen Anne. NRHD

Colonial Revival. NRHD

Colonial Revival. NRHD

Bungalow. NRHD

Bungalow. NRHD

Bungalow. NRHD

Queen Anne. NRHD

Bungalow. NRHD

Bungalow. NRHD

BELLEVIEW CEMETERY AREA

Belleview Cemetery sits at the head of North First Street and is an important example of nineteenth century landscape architecture. It contains many specimen tree forms and interesting funerary sculpture. It also encompasses the Danville National Cemetery with 393 graves of soldiers who died as a result of the Battle of Perryville. The National Cemetery was established in 1868. These turn-of-the-century houses line the street from Lexington Avenue to the cemetery gates. NRHD

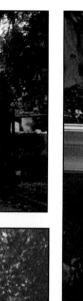

St. Mildred's Court-West Lexington Avenue Historic District

The St. Mildred's Court-West Lexington Avenue Historic District is located west of the commercial core of downtown Danville and is on the north side of Centre College campus. Prior to development, this land was part of a number of small farms on the edge of the original residential and commercial center of town.

Initial development of the area occurred over a fifteen year period beginning in 1912, resulting in remarkable uniformity in design and scale. The predominant architectural styles found in this area include Colonial, Classical, and Tudor Revivals, Foursquare, and Bungalow.

Farris-Humphrey House. *c.1940. West Main at St. Mildred's Court, Danville. Mrs. Farris lived in the Farris-Rochester Mansion on East Main but moved to smaller quarters about 1940. She had this house built with stone from an old mill in Jessamine County. Jennie Rogers School stands on the site of her former house on East Main.*

Bungalow, Dutch Colonial. NRHD

Bungalow. NRHD

An early frame exception on the street. This Greek Revival structure was relocated here about 1900. NRHD

Tudor Revival Bungalow. NRHD

Tudor Revival Bungalow. NRHD

Classical Revival Bungalow. NRHD

Bungalow. NRHD

Bungalow. NRHD

Bungalow. NRHD

Bungalow. NRHD

American Foursquare. NRHD

American Foursquare. NRHD

American Foursquare. NRHD

American Foursquare. NRHD

Bungalow. NRHD

Bungalow with front sleeping porch. NRHD

American Foursquare. NRHD

American Foursquare. NRHD

Bungalow. NRHD

American Foursquare. NRHD

Tudor Revival Bungalow. NRHD

Tudor Revival. NRHD

Craftsman Bungalow. NRHD

House c.1938. West Lexington Avenue, Danville. This two story brick and wood shingle home exhibits unusual Tudor details such as wall dormers, multiple front gables, a brick first story and wood shingled second story, and a steep sloping roof with overhanging eaves which emphasize its height and mass. It was designed by Cincinnati architect Charles Celarius who also designed the Public Library. *NRHD*

Tudor Revival NRHD

Tudor Revival NRHD

Colonial Revival. NRHD

Dutch Colonial on East Lexington. NRHD

Tudor Revival. *Louisville architect V.P. Collins designed this structure in 1915 for developer Minnie G. Turner with an unusual second story overhang, and engaged one story porch, a brick water table course and decoratively applied half-timbering.*

Tudor Revival. NRHD

Colonial Revival. NRHD

Colonial Revival. NRHD

Colonial Revival. NRHD

Colonial Revival. NRHD

Dutch Colonial Revival. NRHD

Colonial Revival. NRHD

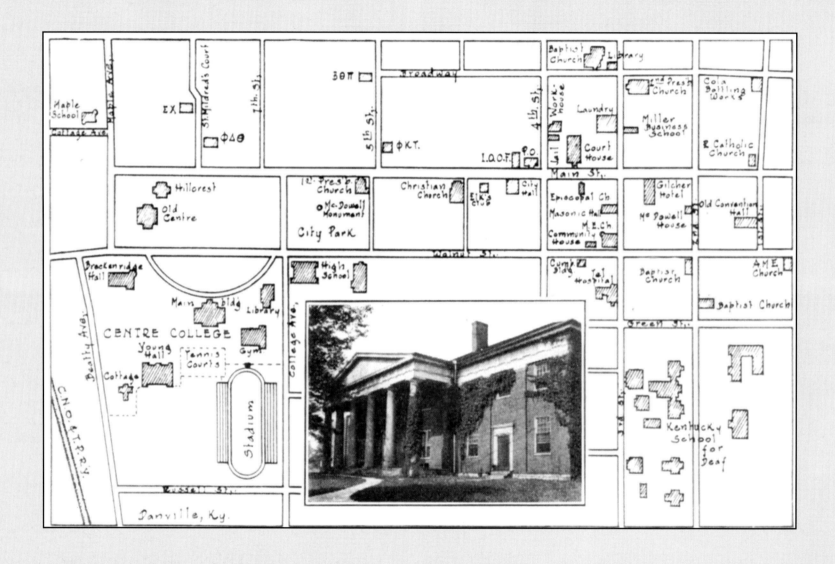

Maple School

Cottage Ave.

Maple Ave.

7th St.

St. Mildred's Court

ΣΧ

ΦΔΘ

5th St.

ΘΘΠ

Broadway

ΦΚΤ.

I.O.O.F.

4th St.

P.O.

Work-house

Jail

Laundry

Court House

Baptist Church

Library

2nd Pres'b Church

Miller Business School

Cola Bottling Works

R Catholic Church

Main St.

Hillcrest

Old Centre

1st Pres'b Church

McDowell Monument

City Park

Christian Church

Elks Club

City Hall

Episcopal Ch.

Masonic Hall

M.E.Ch

Community House

Gilcher Hotel

McDowell House

Old Convention Hall

Walnut St.

Brackenridge Hall

Main bldg

Library

CENTRE COLLEGE

Young Hall

Tennis Courts

Gym

Cottage

Bealty Ave.

C.N.O.&T.P.Ry.

Stadium

High School

College Ave.

Cumb. bldg

Hospital

Baptist Church

A.M.E. Church

Baptist Church

Green St.

Kentucky School for Deaf

Russell St.

Danville, Ky.

CHAPTER VI

Main Streets

Danville's traditional town center encompasses Main Street from Constitution Square to Centre College and the blocks north and south of it. When the early settlers decided to establish the first court in the Kentucky district of Virginia at Crow's Station instead of Harrod's Town, Danville's destiny as an early political, educational and religious center was soon established.

Since Walker Daniel was appointed to secure a location and build a log courthouse, he purchased land from John Crow and laid out the square in its present location in 1784. Taverns, livery stables, general stores and inns soon followed.

To participate in these crucial civic affairs, a settler had to purchase one of Daniel's sixty three lots offered for sale. On the lot, a home at least sixteen feet square with a brick or stone chimney had to be erected.

From 1785 to 1792, when the last of the ten Constitutional Conventions leading to statehood ended, the square was the center of activity of the new town. A Presbyterian meeting house, called Concord, two tav-

erns owned by Grayson and Barbee, a jail and several residences had joined the District Court.

By the early 1800's, Dr. McDowell was performing surgery on Second Street, Daniel McIlvoy was selling salt and general merchandise and the Davenport Inn was open on Main Street.

Centre College welcomed its first class in 1820. During the 1830's and 1840's the Presbyterian and Episcopal Churches, along with the new courthouse were erected near the center of Main Street.

Most of these Federal brick structures marching west of the square had replaced earlier log structures but a disastrous fire struck on Washington's birthday in February 1860. The cause was uncertain but by the morning of the 23rd, the walls of Trinity Church were the only thing standing in the center of the Main Street commercial and residential area. Rebuilding started immediately and a new courthouse was opened in early 1862 only to see it and many other facilities become hospitals after the Battle of Perryville in October of the same year.

By 1875, most of the new buildings had drifted away from the Greek Revival style to Italianate. Many of these edifices still show elements of that period. The two blocks on each side of Main and Third consist of two and three story structures with metal cornices and flat hood moldings over the windows, some with cast iron pilasters. Later buildings show characteristics of Victorian Gothic, Classical Revival, Beaux Arts and Romanesque.

The smaller communities in the county developed into commercial centers as outside influences dictated change. First Shelby City and soon Junction City grew quickly in the late 1800s due to the building of new rail lines through the areas. In addition to stores offering general merchandise, there were passenger depots, freight stations, telegraph offices and hotels.

In Perryville, Merchant's Row was the center of activity where six stores, a doctor's office, a drugstore and a church lined the street in 1860. Several schools and a hotel with a stagecoach stop were within the city boundaries.

As with all our communities, urban and rural, the commercial, religious and educational facilities which have been preserved convey a historic sense of time and place.

The oldest known photograph of Danville, taken in 1875. Dr. Ayres' dentist shop is to the left of Trinity Episcopal Church and the Fields Hotel is on the southwest corner of Fourth and Main. Kentucky School for the Deaf was founded there in 1823 when it was an inn known as the Yellow House.

Perryville

Junction City

Danville

EARLY VIEWS OF MAIN STREET, DANVILLE.

In 1900 Danville's population was around 3500. Establishments selling merchandise were called stores. A shop was a barber or blacksmith shop. A general merchandise store was a department store such as Welsh and Wiseman.

This block of Main Street between Third and Fourth demonstrates the post Civil War transition from Greek Revival to Italianate. All these brick structures have metal cornices and flat hood moldings over the windows. Located in this block through the years has been a bank, a business college, a department store, a Masonic Hall, a pool hall, and an investment firm. NRHD

The Citizens National Bank was founded under the name of the First National Bank of Danville in October 1865. NRL/NRHD

The Boyle Bank and Trust Company at 319 West Main Street, Danville. This building has housed various commercial enterprises including drug stores, jewelry stores, and a photography shop. The Classical Revival style became apparent in 1922 when the stone veneer was applied during its conversion to Boyle Bank and Trust. NRL/NRHD

Welsh and Wiseman Building. *Remodeled c.1915. Northeast corner of Third and Main. NRL/NRHD A general merchandise store which originally opened in the 1840's.*

Northeast corner of Third and Main, prior to 1915.

North side of Main at Fourth Street. The Danville Office Equipment building has been home to a variety of retail businesses, including books, drugs, hardware and office supplies. NRL/NRHD

Activity on Main Street with tight rope exhibitionist.

A handsome group in front of the old Coomer Paint Store, early 1900's.

Two of the four groceries on Main Street.

At right: *The Manhattan Bowling Alley is thought to be the only one of its kind ever to be on Main Street. It provided exercise, lunches, and cigars.*

Far right: *Early furniture store, Dunlap and McGoodwin, at 213 Main Street.*

At left and above: *Two views of Main at Second Street. It was originally J.P. Franks' Department Store, and, later, a movie theater.*

Maple Tree Gallery on Main was built in 1910 and was a millinery shop in 1914. It now has an Art Deco stuccoed edifice with streamlined detailing. NRL/NRHD

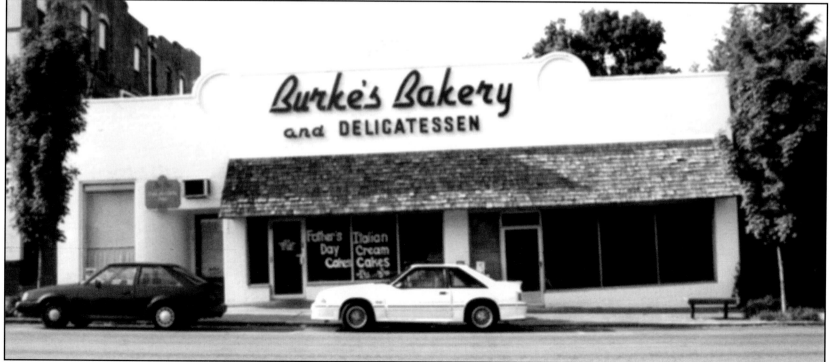

Burke's Bakery. c.1930. East Main Street. A one story, three bay brick building with circular parapets in the Art Deco style. The bakery is an institution on Main Street. NRL

Henson Hotel. *c.1910. Northeast side of Main Street. A three story, five bay brick Colonial Revival structure with brick hood moldings. This 1940's photograph shows the hotel and its neighbors, a movie theatre, a taxi fleet, and the bus depot. The motto on the sign says "Comfort Without Extravagance." NRL*

Ayres Silversmith Shop, which dates prior to 1790, was purchased by brothers Thomas, a silversmith, and Samuel, a dentist, from Dr. Jefferson Polk in 1833. Thomas Ayres made most of the old silver in and around Danville. When he moved to Iowa, George Sharp kept the business. Presently, the building is used as a physician's office. NRL

McIlvoy House. c.1806. As it appeared in 1940. Daniel McIlvoy, who came from Ireland to Kentucky before 1797, owned over 100 acres of Danville proper, north of Main and West of Third. His home was built around 1800 on Main and was used as the Post Office (1829-1832), a bank, and finally as the Bluegrass Garage. It was razed and a professional office now occupies the spot.

McGrorty Drug Store, Southwest corner of Main and Second. Alexander McGrorty came to Danville from Ireland in 1838, and entered into the druggist business with Montgomery and Fry at the corner of Main and Second, often called the Hendren Corner. In 1840, he bought out the partners and remained continuously in business for fifty seven years except in the aftermath of the great fire of 1860 and the Battle of Perryville.

Fox's Livery Stable on Main Street was the largest stable in Central Kentucky, extending through to Walnut Street.

In 1875, Peter Gilcher bought the corner of Third and Main which was to become the "hub" of activity in Danville. He had a building known as Henderson's torn down to make way for his new Gilcher Hotel, which also housed a confectionery and restaurant known as the Gilcher Sweet Shop. A large dining room was on the ground floor along with a kitchen and office. It was built to accommodate traveling salesmen. There were thirty-four rooms for paying guests.

The building was updated in June 1899 when plumbing was added! The bakery and confection shop continued to operate until his death in 1908 when the hotel business was leased to a number of managers. In 1909, the new managers at the Gilcher Hotel opened a second restaurant in the train station, featuring fine food and live music. In March, 1914, the hotel was destroyed by fire due to faulty wiring. *NRL/NRHD*

*Sketch of the new **Gilcher Hotel,** April 1917.*

The Pushin Brothers opened **"The Hub"** department store before 1917.

The Gilcher Hotel was first built on the corner of Third and Main Streets in 1886, however, it burned in 1914. This three-story brick hotel building was rebuilt in the Classical Revival style on this same site.

Above and right: *Farmers National Bank* addition on South Third Street was built in 1903 as a Masonic Building with retail on the first floor, selling meat, groceries, and hardware. It is an eight bay, three story structure with Mansard roof, center gable and stone sills and lintels. *NRL/NRHD*

Below: *The center of the block south of Main between Third and Fourth is a ten bay, two story building with arched brick window hoods and Italianate detailing, c.1880. It has housed hardware, grocery, clothing, and general commercial merchandise. NRL/NRHD*

Above: *The Foley Building.* c.1882. An Italianate seven bay building with elaborate brick corbelling and a metal cornice. The windows are arched and linked with brick hood moldings. It has housed grocery, hardware, and harness stores since 1886. NRL/NRHD

At left: The house on the southeast corner of Main and Fourth was the residence and office of Dr. J.R. Cowan. It was a two story, three bay Classical Revival structure with a central tower, one story porch and balcony. This photo shows how busy the corner of Fourth and Main has always been.

The **R.M. Arnold Carriage Factory** was located behind the Henson Hotel and was operated in the 1870's by Mainwaring Brothers.

Early trade on Walnut.

The livery stable on Fourth Street just south of Main Street, where a bank is now located, was owned and operated by Gaines, Cotton and Reed. In the mid-twentieth century, it housed an antique business owned by Mrs. Zula Hensley.

Above: *Montgomery Hospital.* c.1903. Was built on Fifth Street by Dr. Fayette Montgomery. NRL
At left: The hospital was moved to Walnut Street in 1916 and renamed Ephraim McDowell in 1949.

Above: *The Old Danville Municipal Building,* built in 1916, was razed about 1960 and replaced with the Fire and Police Headquarters we know today.
At right: *Junction City Municipal Building and Post Office.* c.1939. Shelby Street. Built by the W.P.A. NRL

Marshall's Café. *Restaurant on South Fourth Street, now Freddie's, is a one story, three bay structure that has dispensed food and drink for over 60 years.*

Doric Lodge #18. *Two story building on West Walnut, Danville. The lodge was established in 1888, met first on Main, then on Second and finally since 1973 on Walnut in the building that once belonged to the Odd Fellows.*

Italianate. c. 1910. West Main Street. NRHD

Italianate. c. 1910. South Fourth Street.

The Danville Golf Club was organized in 1920 and first located on North Third Street. By the mid 1920's it had moved to the Lexington Road location. The name was changed to Danville Country Club and this clubhouse was constructed. It was remodeled and used until the present one was erected in 1998.

Gwinn Island was created by the flooding of Herrington Lake in 1925 and has always been a fishing camp and popular resort.

The Danville Fairgrounds was located on the corner of the present day intersection of Perryville Road and the US 127 Bypass. It included a horse race and training track and grandstands, and was a most popular wagering spot for gentlemen from 1855 to 1915.

Perryville was laid out in sixty-four town lots in 1815 on the site of Harberson's Station. The Post Office was established in 1816 and the town officially chartered in 1817. The town is located at the junction of the roads from Danville to Springfield and from Harrodsburg to Lebanon. After the Battle of Perryville, the streets were renamed for the commanding generals, with Union names on the west side of the river, since they came from that direction, and Confederate names on the east side as they had approached from that direction. On the west side of Buell Avenue, a commercial section known as Merchants Row overhangs the east bluff of the Chaplin River. These photos show the "Row" in both centuries. *NRL*

Above: *Dr. J.J. Polk Office.* c.1850. Buell Street, Perryville. Dr. Polk, a respected local physician, lived next door and practiced medicine in this small frame office. He treated the wounded after the Battle of Perryville. *NRL*

Penn's Store. c.1850. This store has been in continuous operation for 150 years on the North Rolling Fork River. It is a one story frame building with board and batten siding and a shed-roof porch. Mr. Dick Penn sold merchandise, was the postmaster, and was licensed to practice medicine and dentistry, and to dispense drugs. *NRL*

CHAPTER VII

Churches

Throughout Boyle County and other areas of the Bluegrass, the establishment of church congregations was one of the first tasks to accomplish. The early meeting houses offered a place of worship as well as a place of socialization and educational opportunities.

The first and only congregation in Danville for almost 25 years was that of the Presbyterians. Father David Rice, who also organized Transylvania Academy, was the leader of Concord Presbyterian Church which was built as a meeting house on the Public Square around 1775. In 1778, the congregation moved to the location in what is now McDowell Park. A small brick structure was built about 1812 and the present church in the late 1820's by Robert Russel, Jr. The bell tower was added in the 1850's and in the 1870's remodeling gave us the Victorian Gothic look we have today. The Second Presbyterian Church was organized after the Civil War and met until the mid-20th century.

Across the street on Chapel Lane, now North Fifth Street, the Catholics erected the first brick church about 1810. Daniel McIlvoy, who gave the land, had financial difficulties in the 1820's and could not continue his support of the church. The congregation seems to have disappeared before 1830. The structure immediately became a private dwelling as it continues to be today. Around 1860 Saint Peter and Paul Catholic Church was built in the Gothic Revival style on Main Street. Even though the Catholic Church numbers were slim, parish churches were organized in Junction City, Perryville, and in the knobs. All but the Danville parish has closed.

By the 1820's and 1830's, other denominations joined the religious community. Trinity Episcopal Church, which was also built by Robert Russel, Jr. in 1830, was located in the center of present day Main Street. The First Baptist Church, which first met near the square, moved to its present location on Broadway. It later split into different groups, one going to Lexington Avenue, the second to Green Street, and eventually to Walnut Street. Both the Christian and Methodist congregations have had several locations in the downtown area, as well as in the county.

Church design followed traditional architectural forms and plans. Simple frame or brick structures with gabled-front, nave plans with entrances placed below a central or corner bell tower are often seen in the rural locations of the county. Following ecclesiastical movements nationally and having greater financial stability, churches in town were more sophisticated. From the mid-1800's to the early 1900's, the preference was Gothic Revival, Romanesque or Classical Revival. Fortunately most of these structures are still places of worship today.

THREE EARLY FRAME CHURCHES.

Wilson Chapel. AME Church, Parksville.

Parksville Christian Church. c.1865.

Caldwell Presbyterian Church. c.1828. K 34 W near Parksville Crosspike, and old Caldwell Station. Now a private residence. NRS

Old Salt River Baptist Church. Founded 1789. Salt River Church Road. This frame church was built by the congregation in 1840, on land given by Mr. Joseph Wigham. The church first met on the land of James Harlan until 1818, when James Lillard offered them land after Harlan's death. This was the third location of the church and used until February 1959 when it burned. The congregation moved to the present location on Perryville Road.

Clifton Baptist Church. c.1886. Clifton Road. The church was the nucleus of the Clifton community, established after the Civil War as a freed Negro hamlet. At one time it included a school, dining hall, and cemetery. NRL

Above: *First Baptist Church.* First Street, Perryville. Frame with simple Gothic arched windows. NRL

At right: *Perryville Baptist Church.* This church was organized in 1818 by members who broke away from the Salt River Baptist Church. The group did not have a building until this one was constructed in 1877. This Gothic style church continues to be occupied by the congregation but has been greatly remodeled over the years. In its first rendition, shown here, it was a lovely Gothic Revival building with brick dentils and stone arches over the windows.

The small photo (below) is the reconstructed early building in Constitution Square, in which met the **Concord Presbyterian Church** led by Father David Rice. c.1775. Concord moved west to the proximity of Centre College about 1828. When the congregation split in 1853 due to overcrowding, the West Main Street congregation became First Presbyterian and the new congregation became Second Presbyterian, located on Third Street at Broadway. Both buildings are Church Gothic Revival in the highest form known locally. NRL

At right: *Trinity Episcopal Church.* c.1830. *West Main Street, Danville. The church was organized in 1829 and built in 1831 by Robert Russel, Jr., and the steeple was added in 1842. Even though the interiors had to be reconstructed, it was the only edifice standing on Main Street after the great fire of 1860. NRL*

Far right: *Centenary Methodist Church.* c.1889. *South Third Street, Danville. The first Methodist church built in Danville was a log building constructed in 1789 on this site. It was razed and the present church erected in 1889. NRL*

This photo shows the **First Christian Church**, *Danville, when it was located on the corner of Fourth and Walnut. It was built in 1867 to replace an earlier church destroyed in the great fire of 1860. The church was in this location until 1914, when it moved to West Main. The Gothic Revival building has since been used as a Moose Lodge, a movie theater and apartments.*

The new **First Christian Church**, *Danville, built in 1914 in the new Classical Revival style. This building burned in 1965.*

Saints Peter and Paul Catholic Church. c.1868. *Main Street, Danville. Was built on this land in 1868 and is the oldest Gothic Revival Church in Danville. Elongated Gothic windows, brick buttresses which divides the structure into bays, and stone accent the facade. NRL*

Saint Mary's Catholic Church. (Bank of Perryville/Post Office). *It is a one story painted brick building that is enhanced with a series of arched brickwork along the front parapet wall with a gabled roof just beyond. The main central entry is raised above the sidewalk and is supported by a stone foundation. The building has been used historically for a number of things including a bank and post office. NRL*

Saint Patrick's Catholic Church. c.1885. *Junction City. With the exception of the ramp in front, the church looks much as it did when it was built. NRS*

First Baptist Church. c.1902. on Broadway in Danville. First organized in 1823 by nine members of the Providence Baptist Church on Lancaster Road. A log meeting house was built in 1825 on Broadway. A second church built in 1844 burned and the present Romanesque building completed in 1902. The church also opened the Baptist Female Academy in 1861, which was incorporated into Kentucky College for Women on Lexington Avenue. NRL

St. James A.M.E. Church. c.1882. East Walnut Street, Danville. Congregation was organized in 1872. Building was remodeled in 1924. NRS

These three churches are period revival variations of very early Christian church forms. Built or renovated in the first quarter of the century, they have many features in common: brick masonry, large stained glass arch head windows, wide square towers with louver vents, stone lintels and double entry doors.

Perryville Methodist Church. c.1858. with renovations. *NRL*

Parksville Christian Church. *NRS*

First Christian Church. c.1932. Junction City. *NRL*

At left: *First Baptist Church.* Founded 1846. Walnut Street at Second, Danville. This building was built in 1901 and burned in 1966. Rev. J.E. Wood was pastor for thirty-one years. During his tenure the name was changed from Green Street Baptist to First Baptist Church. NRHD

Below: *Lexington Avenue Baptist Church.* W. Lexington Avenue, Danville. Established 1927, the congregation having split from the First Baptist Church on Broadway. Begun in 1928, the Colonial Revival building was designed by Frankel and Curtis Architects of Lexington and built by a Mr. Foster. The Menelly chimes were given by Mr. John A. Chestnut. NRHD

Chapter VIII

Schools

Since religious sects formed early and learned men came from the East coast and the continent, it is natural that providing for the education of our citizens would be an immediate goal of the early pioneers. Transylvania Academy was chartered in 1785, at the log home of Father David Rice on Buster Pike. Rice was one of the thirteen trustees of lands vested by the Commonwealth of Virginia for the purpose of establishing seminaries on the growing western frontier. Classes were held in the log house and perhaps in a stone structure for about four years when it was decided by the board to move to Lexington, a more urban area. Thus the academy, which later became Transylvania University, was the first college west of the Allegheny Mountains.

From these humble beginnings, Danville became known as a center of education and culture. Centre College was chartered in 1819 and Robert Russel built its first facility, now known as "Old Centre" in 1820. A law school, as well as a theological seminary, were located for a time on Centre's campus. Military schools, such as Hogsett Academy, and schools for girls, Danville Female Academy and Caldwell College, were formed. Some of these included primary grades through college. In the county, Perryville had its own private schools. The Ewing Institute, Elmwood School and Elmwood Academy were established in the 1800's.

In 1823 the Kentucky School for the Deaf was established in Danville. This was probably because one of Elias Barbee's daughters was deaf and he had heard of Dr. Gallaudet's schools on the east coast. Barbee introduced the bill to the state legislature in 1822 and the Centre College trustees undertook to establish the first state deaf school in the nation. It first met in the Yellow House, an inn on the corner of Main and Fourth Street, before moving to South Second Street.

The Civil War and financial panics through the last years of the 19th century saw many of these schools close or consolidate. It continued to be understood that education was important, but many could not afford tuition or room and board. The public or common schools, as they were called, struggled because the agrarian community was slow to vote to raise taxes to support them. Most of the villages in the county had simple one room school houses by the late 1800's. The towns of Junction City, Perryville, and Forkland had their own secondary schools.

The African-American leaders of the community worked to establish a public school after the Freedman's Bureau School closed in the 1870's. They took over the Bureau's old building near Stanford Avenue and opened it soon after. The first teacher, Professor John Bate, stayed for almost forty years. During the early 1900's, Bate School was named for him. Prior to that, Willis Russell, a freed slave of Richard Craddock, opened his log house to educate black children.

Danville and Boyle County continue to be recognized in the arena of education for their outstanding facilities and nationally renown educators throughout the 20th century.

Old Danville High School. c.1917. *West Walnut Street, Danville. A one story craftsman type building, razed in mid-1960's to make way for the Norton Center.*

Broadway School. c.1900. *Stone and brick structure with stone arches and keystones, and a bell tower. This building burned in 1950.*

Old Bate School. c.1900. *A later photo showing additions, including a gymnasium.*

Early brick school in Constitution Square.

Hogsett Academy *was a private military school in the late nineteenth century. The Romanesque building had a stone foundation and large corner tower. It sat on Maple Avenue until Toliver School was built in its place in 1929.*

Edna L. Tolliver School. *c.1929. Was known in the beginning as the Maple Avenue School. This form is Classical Revival with giant portico, columns, and bell tower. NRL*

A replica of the first school house at Forkland Community center – single pen rectangular one-story log building.

Above: *Forkland School.* This tall, brick, seven bay wide school building was constructed in 1928 to replace the nine one room schools including three in Casey County and the three room Sycamore School. The Sycamore School had replaced the original log school house. The first class graduated from Forkland High School in 1930. The gymnasium was built in 1938 of Kentucky limestone quarried from the top of Mitchellsburg Knob with construction help from the Works Project Administration.

At right: *White Oak School.* Early twentieth century one-room school.

The Ewing Female Institute. *c.1856. Fifth Street, Perryville. This two story, three bay, Federal style structure was built to house an antebellum girls' boarding school, founded in 1840. It was operated in conjunction with Harmonia College. The building was occupied by troops during the Battle of Perryville. Harmonia never reopened after the war. The institute continued to operate and prospered until about 1915, when it became a high school. It has been a private residence for many decades. NRL*

Elmwood Academy. c.1842. Fourth Street in Perryville. This home was built by a prominent merchant, J.A. Burton and saw use as a shelter for the injured during the Battle of Perryville. It was converted and used as the Elmwood Academy from 1891 to 1925.

In the mid-1800's, the education of women was becoming increasingly important. Several academies, Henderson, Caldwell, Bell and the Danville Female Institute were established and merged on both sides of Lexington Avenue, culminating in the creation of the Kentucky College for Women. All the remaining buildings were razed in 1960's when Danville High School was moved to the site.

At right: *A wonderful panoramic view of the* **Danville Female Institute** *and the girls in all their splendor.* Below: **Henderson Institute for Women.** *C.1859.*

Kentucky College for Women. *Formerly Caldwell College, was finally Women's Department of Centre College. Morgan Hall was a large Italianate residence building with a 1 1/2 story Gothic Revival porch.*

*These buildings, East Hall, West Hall, and Morgan Hall comprised the classrooms and dormitories of the **Kentucky College for Women.***

Kentucky School for the Deaf was established by the state legislature in 1823 and has been located on South Second Street since 1826. These buildings from its early history, represent a range of architectural styles from Greek Revival through Italianate. c.1840-1900. All these great old buildings have been razed, leaving only Jacobs Hall.

Warwick Hall. c.1843. Razed 1958.

Old Chapel. c.1840. Razed in the 1960's.

Early view. **Jacob's Hall** *on left.*

Dormitories for boys and girls.

Dudley Hall. *Razed in the 1970's.*

Kerr Hall. *Razed in the 1970's.*

Dormitory for boys. *c.1888.*

CENTRE COLLEGE

Centre College was chartered by the Kentucky Legislature on January 1, 1819. Old Centre was built in 1820 in the Greek Revival style and is perhaps the oldest college building west of the Allegheny Mountains. Centre's history has been intertwined with other schools because of its public and religious affiliations. Centre had a medical school between 1833 and 1857. Danville Theological Seminary began in 1853 and was on this campus until 1901.

A late nineteenth century view of old Centre

Above and lower right:
Two views of Old Main, an early Classical Revival example. c.1871. Was in continuous useuntil it was razed in the 1960's.

Boyle Humphrey Gymnasium, in the Romanesque form, was the finest gym in Kentucky in 1905 and later was the site of the first boy's high school state basketball tournament.

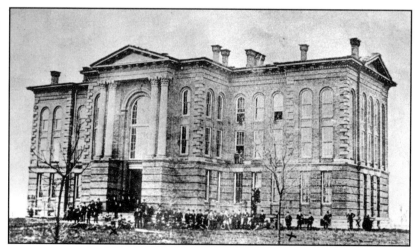

First Sayre Library. c.1862. This octagon form is rare nationwide, but especially in Kentucky.

Breckinridge Hall. c.1892. Built to house the theological seminary, it became part of the core of Centre's campus when the seminary moved to Louisville in 1900.

Second Sayre Library. c.1893. Although larger and the Romanesque form is pleasing, it is the opinion of the authors that the new library could in no way compare to the first one for sheer beauty and whimsical form.

CHAPTER IX

Industry and Travel

Early transportation systems in Boyle County during the settlement period consisted of natural pathways established along buffalo trails. These pathways connected manufacturing sites, including mills and salt works, and transportation sites such as river crossings and ferries.

Along major regional routes, occasional stage coach stations, taverns and inns provided food, lodging, animal care and docile interaction to both traveler and local alike. Springs located along these early routes were used by all who traveled them. The faint road bed of the Wilderness Road remains near the large cave spring that provides piped water to the C.C. Moore Farm.

One early important route extended along the Salt River. James Harlan established Harlan's Station along the Salt River trail, and John Irvin established his station south of Harlan's Station along the river closer to the salt works. Today, the Salt River Road is defined by paired dry-laid rock fences on either side of this narrow asphalt covered roadbed.

Following the initial settlement period, the establishment of new and improved transportation routes became increasingly important. Many of these roads were privately owned as toll pikes or roads. The tollhouses were located approximately five miles apart along these roads but none are believed to remain in Boyle County today. During the Antebellum Period, secondary roads were often defined by dry-laid rock fences. Many were the work of Irish and Scot stone masons who immigrated to the Bluegrass in the early-through mid-19th century, bringing their traditional rock building practices with them. Today, these rock fences define farm fields, barn lots, property lines and road edges.

With the expansion of railways after the War Between the States and workforce changes wrought by industrial development, population began a gradual shift from rural to urban areas.

The locations of railroad stations often became small urban communities such as Junction City, Shelby City, Parksville and Mitchellsburg, with businesses that linked town and farm and provided services for rail passengers and commercial freight.

Danville became a major link in the Southern railroad system after the construction of High Bridge over the Kentucky River in 1877. The first station built on the west end of Walnut Street was a wood-frame structure with a hipped roof and platform. Located on the west side of the tracks was the steam powered Potts, Proctor and Company Eclipse Roller mills. The Danville Roller Mills and Grain Elevator were nearby on the Perryville Pike. A warehouse and grocery, expanding the commercial nature of the area, was built on the northeast corner of Harding and Walnut. North of the train station was the Samuel Harding Lumber Company. Various building's housed sawing and storage functions of the company.

East of Harding Street, the Cogar and Davis Warehouse for hemp hackling and storage was built. A freight depot was added to the southern portion of the trans-portation complex. By 1908 the Harding Lumber Company facility had been bought and expanded by the Danville Lumber Company. Buildings contained a planing mill, office and steam-dry room. The present brick depot with its overhanging eaves and high-hipped roof replaced the original one. On the corner of Walnut and Harding, a two-story brick warehouse was built for the storage and sale of grain, hemp, and feed. A restaurant, Western Union Office, and express office were added to the area, and the tobacco warehouses were built.

The warehouse buildings left in the area are multiple story brick structures with flat roofs and stone foundations. The facades have very little ornamentation, consistent with the nature of their use.

The Warehouse District provides visible evidence of Danville's late 19th and early 20th century prominence as a rail transportation hub which attracted industry and commerce and provided for wide distribution of locally grown products.

The **Water Works Power House,** *located at the junction of the Dix River and Clark's Run, was built of stone with a slate roof and heated by steam, circa 1893. Razed.*

Above left: *Danville Lumber Company,* near railroad yard.
Above right: *The Stand Pipe.* c.1904. Early water storage located at the water company near Lexington Avenue, Danville.
At right: Grain elevator near railroad station, Danville.

Danville Planning Mill. c.1908. *Near railroad yard.*

*Heat, light, and laundry plant at **Kentucky School for the Deaf.** c.1912.*

Danville Lumber and Manufacturing Company.

Danville Ice and Coal Company.
Perryville Road.

Dillehay Brick Company

Above: *C.T. Armstrong Steam Mill.* *US 68, Perryville. Was constructed in 1876 and remains a two story brick building with a one stoory side addition support by a stone foundation. The large square brick chimney stacks are still visible. NRL*
At left: *Danville Roller Mill, near railroad yard.*

Above: *Mills House.* c.1880. Walnut Street. This brick Italianate home became part of the development of the warehouse district. And was sometimes used as an office. NRHD

At left: *Coffee Cup Restaurant,* on Walnut Street near the train depot was built circa 1900. This two story brick structure was a popular gathering place for employees in the warehouse district. NRL/NRHD

Cogar Hemp & Grain Warehouses on Harding Street in Danville, were built by George Cogar in 1902 for storing and processing hemp and gain. They are constructed of brick and are now part of the Centre College Campus. NRL/NRHD

The Danville Train Depot, built in 1908, is a one story brick structure on a stone foundation with a two story central rounded portion and a one story porch supported by long brackets that extend around the structure. The first train station was built in 1886. After the construction of High Bridge over the Kentucky River in 1877, an agricultural complex grew up in the area, and the original train station was replaced by this one. The train depot was the center of the transportation and industrial hub that developed. An excellent example of a transition from the Romanesque to the Craftsman style. *NRL*

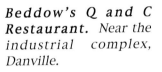

Beddow's Q and C Restaurant. Near the industrial complex, Danville.

Goresburg was a railroad town which catered to travelers, railroad employees, and their families. The town's name evolved to Danville Junction and eventually Junction City, with a post office, three hotels, a municipal building, churches, a school, and various commercial establishments.

Railroad Signal Tower, *Junction City, c. 1900.*

Cozatt Telegraph Station, *Parksville.*

C. 1950.   **Junction City Railroad Station.**   *C.1912.*

Green and Crescent Freight Depot, *Junction City.*

Railroad Tower, North of Danville.

Railroad Section House, *Wards Branch Road. Section houses housed employees charged with maintenance and oversight of sections of track.*

Early water tower. Parksville.

Junction City was a busy place in the early 1900's for travelers and salesmen, with two railroads which crossed in town. During its heyday, it had three hotels: the Rosel Hotel, the Trible House, and the McCollum House. The McCollum House was located on the southwest side and the Rosel Hotel on the northwest side with the depot on the northeast corner. Many times, all three hotels were filled and people had to be taxied to Danville for accommodations. As automobiles became more plentiful and roads improved in the 1920's and 1930's, small town hotels began to fade away. The Rosel Hotel continued to operate until the mid-1960's

Rosel Hotel. Junction City. NRL

Hotel Routin. Junction City.

Hotel McCollum. Junction City.

Rosel Hotel and Restaurant. Junction City. NRL

*Two views of the **Boyle House Hotel**. c.1865 & 1869. Corner of US 150 W and US 68, Perryville.*

The automobile brought profound and permanent changes to city streets, county roads and bridges, and the delivery of goods and services related to the motor vehicle. Livery stables were replaced by service stations and horse drawn hacks became taxi cabs.

At left: *Coffee Pot Service Station.* US 127, Shelby City. Built by Floyd Abbott. Razed 1953.
Below: *Art Deco Service Station.* North Third Street, Danville.

The **Old King's Mill and covered bridge** were located at the Dix River on the Lexington Road before being submerged in 1925 by the formation of Herrington Lake. This mill was built before 1800 by Peter Belles to grind wheat, corn, and other small grain. The 165 foot covered bridge was built late in 1863 by the Danville, Lancaster, and Nicholasville Turnpike Company to shorten the trip to Lexington. A previous bridge had been burned by Confederate troops in April 1863.

Chenault Bridge. *c.1925. Old KY 34 E. Is near the site on the Dix River of the old King's Mill and covered bridge. This was the main route to Lexington until late 1992 when the new road and bridge opened.*

Iron Bridge over Hanging Fork Creek. NRS

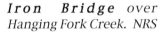

Above left: *The Clifton Road Culvert is a mid-nineteenth century stone masonry bridge spanning an unnamed drainage that falls to the Dix River in eastern Boyle County. This structure was part of the original alignment of the Clifton Road, a nineteenth century route that led through the African-American community of Clifton down to a ferry crossing the Dix River. NRL*

Above right: *The Mitchellsburg Louisville and Nashville (L&N) Railroad Culvert is the crossing of L&N railroad over Buck Creek. This brick and stone culvert, constructed circa 1866, is situated beneath a remaining portion of the L&N alignment and consists of masonry arch of linestone and brick with a stone foundation and stone retention walls. The L&N Rialroad employed local laborers and masons to build the structure under the supervision of the L&N engineers, using locally quarried stone and fired brick. This culvert influenced later rock masonry structures in the county, such as the stone bridge over Chaplin Creek. NRL*

At right: *An interesting stone culvert under KY 1822.*

*Early log dependency at **Wilson's Station**. KY 34 W. NRL*

*Log dependency at **Joseph McDowell house**. US 150 W. NRS*

*Log quarters at **Granite Hill**. c.1810. KY 52 E. NRL*

*Log quarters at **Old Crow**. Stanford Road. NRL*

CHAPTER X

— *Dependencies* —

It is not easy to date or to estimate the importance of the barns and other out-buildings that we here call dependencies. The first settlers must have found them an immediate necessity for the protection of livestock and the storage and safety of crops and food after harvest. The earliest such structures were obviously log and as with dwellings, were followed quickly by ones of stone and brick.

Small buildings soon accompanied the springs that provided water and earliest refrigeration. Underground cellars extended the life of fruits and vegetables while smoke houses allowed for preservation of meat.

The primarily agriculture structures in this chapter include barns for tobacco, cattle and horses (even a 200 year old pony barn), feeders for cattle and tool sheds.

Both on the farms and in town we found tenant and slave quarters, carriage houses and offices.

We offer these interesting and utilitarian buildings as a fitting conclusion to our study.

*Frame dependency at **T.B. Bright** farm. KY 34 E. NRL*

*Dependency at the **Vermillion House** on Salt River Church Road. NRL*

At right: *Frame feeder at **James P. Mitchell Farm**. c.1855. NRS*
Below: *Tenant quarters at **Nimrod Buster farm**. c.1876. Buster Pike. NRL*

At left: *Log slave house at the* **Ludwig house** *on Salt River Church Road.* NRS

Below: *Log barn at the* **Field's farm** *on Salt River Church Road.* NRS

Log slave houses at the **Field's farm** *on Salt River Church Road.* NRS

Bank barn with stone foundation. Bull Lane. NRS

*Antebellum barn at **Nimrod Buster farm**. Buster Pike. NRL*

*Horse barn converted for show cattle at **"Grasslands"**. Bluegrass Pike. NRS*

*Horse barn on the old **Bradshaw farm**. US 127 S.*

*Horse barn at **Granite Hill**. c.1906. KY 52 E. NRL*

*Horse barn with stone foundation at **Cambus Kenneth farm**. US 127 By-pass. NRL*

Dependency at **Randolph-Mock farm.** *c.1800. Gwinn Island Rd. NRL*

Dependency at **Randolph-Mock farm.** *c.1800. Gwinn Island Rd. NRL*

Cellar at **Grasslands.** *Bluegrass Pike. NRS*

*Dependency at the **Durham farm**. US 150 W. NRS*

*Original cabins at **Aliceton Campgrounds**. Ward's Branch Rd. The Aliceton Camp Meeting Ground in far western Boyle county is on a parcel of land deeded for the exclusive use as a place for religious camp meetings, which continue to be held there every July. Buildings include a meeting house, cafeteria, cabins, and wash house. NRL*

*Antebellum dependency at the **Karrick-Parks house**. Buell Street, Perryville. NRL*

Tenant House at **Harlan-Bruce far***m. c.1920. Chrisman Lane. NRL*

Quarters at **Durham farm.** *c.1827. US 150 W. NRS*

Quarters at **Grasslands.**
Bluegrass Pike. NRS

Barn at the **Vermillion farm.** *c.1839. Salt River Church Road. NRL*

Coach house and quarters on West Main, Danville.

Pony barn on the **Logan Caldwell farm.** *c.1800. Irvin Road. NRL*

Relocated frame one-room school at the **Vermillion farm** *on Salt River Church Road.*

Dependency on N. Fifth Street, Danville.

Stone cellar under the driveway at **Dr. William Harlan house.** *Chrisman Lane. NRS*

Stone spring house at **Nimrod Buster farm.** c.1876. Buster Pike. NRL

Stone ice house at **Springhill.** c.1858. US 150 E. NRL

Stone spring house at the **Logan Caldwell farm.** c.1858. Irvin Road. NRL

Cellar with stone front at the **C.T. Worthington farm.** c.1855. Bluegrass Pike. NRL

At right: *Dependency at* **Grasslands.** *Bluegrass Pike. NRS*
Below: *Doctor's office at* **Forest Hill.** *c.1814. KY 34 E. NRL*

Slave quarters at the **R.L.Salter house.** *c.1830. Dogwood Drive, Danville. NRS*

*Dependencies, connected to one another and to the house at **Old Crow**. The oldest section is far left. Smoke house is in the center. All ceiling beams are cherry. Stanford Road, Danville. NRL*

*Brick smoke house at the **Mary Simpson Oldham home** on US 150 W. NRL*

*Brick smoke house at **Springhill**. c.1855. US 150 E. Mr. Lillard locked her favorite horse inside when the calvary came looking for good mounts during the war. NRL*

Above left: *Brick spring house at* **Cambus Kenneth farm.** *c.1800. US 127 By-pass. NRL*

Above right: *Brick tenant house with ginger-bread at* **Cambus Kenneth farm.** *US 127 By-pass. NRL*

At right: *Two story brick servants quarters at* **Cambus Kenneth farm.** *c.1875. US 127 By-pass. NRL*

Brick dependency at **Todd-Cheek House.** *North Third Street, Danville.*

Large dairy barn. Stanford Road, Danville.

Horse barn on the **Clemens Caldwell farm.** *c.1898. Maple Avenue at US 127 By-pass.*

Brick dependency at **McClure-Barbee House.** *South Fourth Street, Danville. NRL*

*Large tobacco barn and crib at **Helm-Gentry farm**. NRS*

*Brick quarters (right) and standpipe for water system (left) at the **Helm-Gentry farm**. US 127 N. NRL*

This last picture is an early postcard of the courthouse, including the horse-watering trough, immortalized in the 1954 novel, <u>Iron Baby Angel</u>, by Charles McDowell.

This beloved landmark stood as a sentinel on Main Street at the turn of the century. Any important news or gossip could be ascertained daily from the street loafers near the fountain. Around 1910 it was dismantled due to the popularity of the "horseless carriage."

Anyone fortunate enough to find a rare copy of this novel will certainly gain insight into the early days of Danville and discover the legend of the iron angels.

Afterword

We again thank each and every property owner, source and participant for the generosity that provided us with information. We shamelessly snapped up every morsel, made it our own and attempted to find the truth, at a distance of up to 200 years. For our mistakes, we apologize.

Lack of space did not allow us to include every worthy structure and we hope that a second volume may someday grow from this one.

The Book Committee

Our special thanks to:

- All the antique show volunteers for help with fundraising.

- A. Jack May for allowing us the use of his sketches.

- Farmer's Bank for use of materials from their scrapbook.

- Barbara May for sharing her family's extensive historical collection.

- Danville Office Equipment for technical support.

- Don Hamner for errands well performed.

Historical References

Amos, Christine and Bradley, Amanda. *Historic Resources of Boyle County, Kentucky.* National Register of Historic Places, 1996.

Breeding, Mary C. *St.Mildred's Court - West Lexington Avenue Historic District.* National Register of Historic Places. 1993.

Brown, Richard C. *A Histoty of Danville and Boyle County, Kentucky, 1774-1992.* Danville, Kentucky: Bicentennial Books, 1992,

Collins, Lewis. *History of Kentucky.* Lewis Collins, Maysville, Kentucky 1847.

Cronan, Mary. *Harlan's Station (James Harlan Stone House)* National Register Nomination. 1976.

Cronan-Oppel, Mary, *Three Gothic Villas.* National Register Nomination, 1976.

Fackler, Calvin Morgan. *Early Days in Danville,* Louisville: The Standard Printing Co., Inc. 1941.

Fackler, Calvin Morgan. *Historic Homes of Boyle County, Kentucky, and Three Courthouses.* The Danville and Boyle County Historical Society, Danville, Kentucky. 1959.

Lancaster, Clay. *Antebellum Architecture in Kentucky.* Lexington, Kentucky The University Press of Kentucky. 1991.

Murray-Wooley, Carolyn. *Early Stone Buildings of Central Kentucky.* Thematic Resources Nomination, National Register of Historic Places. 1983.

Newcomb, Rexford. *Architrecture in Old Kentucky.* University of Illinois, Urbana, Illinois. 1953.

Powell, Helen. *Multiple Resources of Danville, Kentucky.* National Register Nomination. 1984.

Worsham, Gibson. *Boyle County Survey Summary Report.* Boyle County Landmark Trust and Kentucky Heritage Council. 1991.

Glossary

Antebellum: Before the War Between the States, 1820 to 1860.

Bay: A vertical division of a building containing an opening or stack of openings.

Bracketed: Deep eaves upheld by a series of supports.

Carpenters Gothic: Gothic Revival expressed in wood.

Colonial Revival: Twentieth century recreation of early Federal styles. Used 1900 through 1940.

Corinthian: Classical columns distinguished by acanthus ornaments on the heads,

Dog-trot: A covered breezeway between two pens of a log structure.

Doric: Columns characterized by heavy channeled shafts and plain heads.

Early plans:

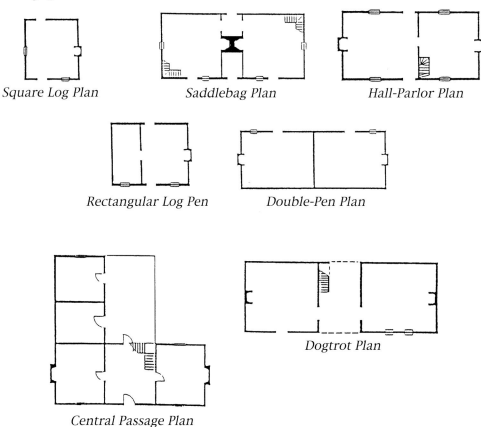

Square Log Plan   *Saddlebag Plan*   *Hall-Parlor Plan*

Rectangular Log Pen   *Double-Pen Plan*

Central Passage Plan   *Dogtrot Plan*

Facade: The face or vertical plane of a building.

Federal: Building style characterized by clean rectangular lines, low-pitched roofs, and simple ornamentation. Used 1720 to 1820, approximately.

Folk Victorian: Local interpretation of Victorian styles.

Gable: The triangular space at the end of a pitched roof.

Gothic Revival: In the style of the architecture of the late middle ages, characterized by pointed arches, vertical lines and elaborate ornamentation. Used 1830 to 1860, approximately.

Greek Revival: A classical style inspired by antique Greek buildings and used in America from 1820 to 1860, approximately, making primary use of central pediments and large columned porches.

Hipped Roof: One that slopes inward from all sides.

Hood Molding: An ornamental shelter over a door or window.

Ionic: Classic columns characterized by voluted heads.

Italianate: A building style taking inspiration from the simplest Italian forms, distinguished primarily by bracketed eaves. Used 1840 to 1880, approximately.

Pediment: A triangular gable,

Pen: A room or storage space in a log structure.

Pilaster: An upright form projecting from a wall and resembling a flattened column.

Post Bellum: After the War Between the States, 1865 to 1899.

Queen Anne: "Victorian" as we know it, interpreted in steep gables, tall chimneys, and high ornamentation. Used 1860-1910, approximately.

Romanesque: Buildings ornamented with horizontal bands of various materials, stone trim and tile roofs. Used 1880 to 1920,

Settlement: Historical period, in Kentucky, 1774 to 1820.

Transom: A window over a door.

Tudor Revival: A style reminiscent of the English cottage, distinguished by half-timbering, brick and stucco, leaded glass windows and slate roofs. Used 1920 to 1940.

Index

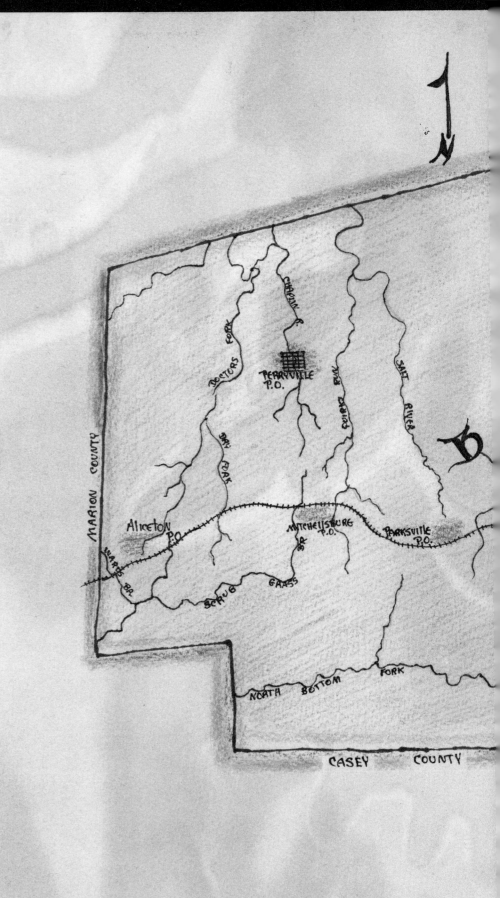